Early Settlements

AMERICAN HISTORIC PLACES

Early Settlements

Ray Spangenburg and Diane K. Moser

Facts On File, Inc.

American Historic Places: *Early Settlements*

Copyright © 1998 by Ray Spangenburg and Diane K. Moser

Facts On File, Inc.
11 Penn Plaza
New York, NY 10001

Library of Congress Cataloging-in-Publication Data

Spangenburg, Ray, 1939–
    Early settlements / Ray Spangenburg and Diane K. Moser.
        p.   cm.—(American historic places)
    Includes bibliographical references (p.) and index.
    ISBN 0-8160-3405-2 (alk. paper)
        1. Historic sites—United States. 2. Human settlements—United
States—History. 3. United States—History, Local.
I. Spangenburg, Ray, 1939–   . II. Title. III. Series.
E159.M68   1998
973—dc21   97-27453

Facts On File books are available at special discounts when purchased in bulk quantities for businesses, associations, institutions or sales promotions. Please call our Special Sales Department in New York at (212) 967-8800 or (800) 322-8755.

You can find Facts On File on the World Wide Web at http://www.factsonfile.com

Text design by Cathy Rincon
Cover design by Dorothy Wachtenheim
Layout by Robert Yaffe
Illustrations on pages vi, 10, 18, 29, 33, 41, 53, 63, 64, 84, 90, 102, and 117 by Jeremy Eagle

Printed in the United States of America

RRD FOF 10 9 8 7 6 5 4 3 2 1

This book is printed on acid-free paper.

To the ancestors of the Crow Nation,

to the Spangenburgs and the Von Buseks,

the Moodys and the Tituses,

the Notsons, the Nelsons, and the Swaffords,

the Jakob Moser family,

and to all the rest of the settlers from all over the world

who came before us to this land

to build a better life

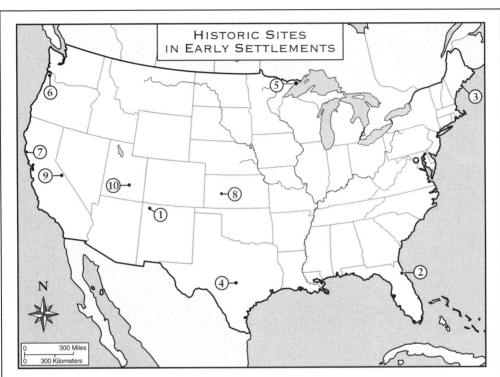

HISTORIC SITES IN EARLY SETTLEMENTS

1 **Aztec Ruins National Monument: Pueblo homes of the Ancient Ones**

2 **St. Augustine and Castillo de San Marcos: first permanent European settlement and its fort**

3 **Colonial Pemaquid: a village frozen in time**

4 **San Antonio Missions National Historic Park: a meeting of two cultures**

5 **Grand Portage National Monument: voyageur rendezvous**

6 **Fort Clatsop: Lewis and Clark's Western campground**

7 **Fort Ross State Historic Park: Russian trading outpost on the Pacific**

8 **Fort Larned: protecting the Santa Fe Trail**

9 **Bodie State Historic Park: Gold Rush ghost town**

10 **Fruita Orchards: rural pioneer village**

CONTENTS

PREFACE TO THE SERIES

History doesn't have to be dry or stuffy. And it isn't exclusively about military skirmishes and legislative proclamations—they make up only a small part of it. History is the story of life events that happened to people who cared as passionately about their lives as we care about ours. And it's the story of events that often continue to shape and influence our lives today. But getting to the human side of these stories isn't always easy. That's why there's nothing like visiting the place where an event actually occurred to get the feel of what it all meant.

The study of historic places—what happened at a particular site and how the lives of the people there were affected—has emerged as a great way to approach history, to "relive" the experience and open up to the immense diversity of American culture. Every community and region is rich in such places—places that highlight real stories about real people and events. Even if you can't actually visit such a place, the next best thing is to go there through pictures and words. Use this book and the other books in this series as jumping-off points and look around your community for places where you can experience the world of the people who once lived in your own region—and begin exploring!

◆ ◆ ◆

Each volume in this series explores a different aspect of U.S. history by focusing on a few select places. This book takes a look at early settlements in the United States from the time of the early Pueblo communities to Spanish explorers and English settlers; and from the first explorations westward to the gold rush towns and rural communities of the West. Of course, choosing exactly which places to focus on in each book was one of the most difficult tasks of this project. We limited our choices to sites that had either been restored or maintained in authentic historic condition—most are National Historic Landmarks, chosen by the U.S. government to be preserved for their historic significance. We also tried to include examples from a wide variety of locations, events and experiences, types of sites, and time periods. We then limited our selections to just a few. But many other fascinating places exist throughout the country, and that's why we mentioned other related sites at the end of some chapters (under Exploring Further) and added a list of additional sites at the back of the book (More Places to Visit).

Each chapter begins with information about the site (At a Glance). Then we explore the place—what it's like and who lived there, how the place related to that person's life and work, and what it's like to visit there today. We also look closely at one feature of the site in "A Close-Up" section, followed by a section recapping how the site came to be a protected historic site (Preserving It for the Future). A list of books and other resources concludes each chapter (Exploring Further), directing readers to either a broader or closer view of the early settlements in the United States.

Exploring historic sites not only provides a way to experience past events with fresh vividness and immediacy, it also offers a way of seeing the past through new eyes, through the eyes of those who lived it. For this adventure—and it can prove to be a lifetime adventure—this series will have accomplished its purpose if it provides the springboard for future explorations. In the words of an old Gaelic greeting, "May the wind be always at your back and may the road rise up to meet you," as you travel down these avenues of historical experience.

ACKNOWLEDGMENTS

Many people all over the country have generously given of their time and expertise to help us make this book better, and we'd like to thank them all, including: Henry Day and Barbara Stanislawski at the National Park Service Intermountain Cultural Resource Center, Tracy Bodner at Aztec Ruins, Sheila McDonald at the State of Maine Bureau of Parks and Recreation, John Sage at Grand Portage, Curt Johnson at Fort Clatsop, Daniel F. Murley at Fort Ross, George Elmore at Fort Larned, and Mark Pupich formerly at Bodie State Historic Park. At Facts On File, special thanks to our editor, Nicole Bowen, for her steady professionalism and incomparable commitment to excellence; to line editor Phil Koslow; copy editor Faith Gabriel; map artist Jeremy Eagle; and our former editor, James Warren, who helped us conceptualize the series. We'd also like to take this opportunity to thank Linda Allen for her years of moral support and friendship.

INTRODUCTION

The earliest settlements on the North American continent didn't begin with the Europeans or with long and arduous ocean voyages. They began instead much earlier with an influx of people using an unusual land route that was as arduous as the routes taken years later by European sailors and explorers.

More than 13,000 years ago, the great freeze known as the Ice Age caused the level of the ocean to drop—because so much of the earth's water was tied up in ice. When that happened, a bridge of land appeared between Siberia and the western shores of Alaska. At just about the same time, humans had begun to migrate into the vast reaches of Siberia, and they probably pursued the game animals that also crossed the land bridge across what is now the Bering Strait. From Alaska, humans moved southward into the wilderness of the North American continent, following the game and the signs of better weather.

As a result, when Europeans such as the Vikings, Italians, and Spanish began to cross the Atlantic Ocean, they were surprised to find a "New World"—but it was only new to them. To the American Indians, it was already home, and had been for thousands of years.

The earliest Indians were hunter-gatherer nomadic peoples who at first rarely settled in one place, although archaeologists have found traces of intermittent communities dating back as far as 9000 B.C.E. (before common era). Petroglyphs and pictographs in New Mexico date back as far as A.D. 800. And the great mounds of Cahokia in Illinois were built as early as A.D. 700. In Chaco Canyon, New Mexico, there are traces of pueblos built as long ago as A.D. 600, with the peak of this culture coming in the 1100s, when the Chacoan "suburb" or outlier known as Aztec Ruins was built.

Also in the 1100s, Viking ships began to nose along the eastern shores of North America, but little evidence indicates that they built any communities here in those earliest days. Four centuries later, Spanish explorers began to arrive to the south, with the expedition led by Ponce de León among the first. By 1565 the Spanish had established their first permanent settlement, in Florida, at what is now St. Augustine—much before the English arrived at Roanoke (1584), Jamestown (1607), or Plymouth Rock (1620).

By 1610, when English settlers first began building a community on the Pemaquid River in Maine, the Spanish had taken a strong hold in Florida. By the end of the 17th century, they had begun to develop a chain of missions across much of the Southwest, including the missions in San Antonio.

The French had a strong interest in North American riches as well, and they staked out claims in Canada to the north and in Louisiana along the Gulf of Mexico. Continually in conflict with the English in Canada, they engaged many Indian tribes as allies and waged a series of wars (1689–1763), which involved many settlers until the English emerged victorious and took control of Canada. Nonetheless, French *voyageurs*—fur trappers who traveled the rivers of the north—continued to ply their trade, and they have left their traces in the United States at places such as Grand Portage, Minnesota, a rendezvous point founded in 1768.

But by 1803, with even greater problems looming at home, the French decided to sell their vast holdings in the heart of the continent, known as Louisiana. The buyer was the young nation, known as the United States, which had recently broken off from England. Once they had purchased Louisiana, the new owners needed to explore what they had acquired and stake their claim by making their presence felt. So Meriwether Lewis and William Clark set out from St. Louis with an exploration party in 1804, traveling some 3,700 miles to the Pacific Ocean, where they spent the winter of 1805–06. There they built the fort known today as Fort Clatsop. It was a key outpost, considerably overstretching the agreed-upon extent of the Louisiana Purchase and setting the nation's sights on the Far West.

Meanwhile, just eight years later, the Russian-American Company staked out a claim on the coast of (Alta) California, just north of what was then a vast Spanish territory extending up from Mexico. The new Russian outpost was known as Fort Ross (1811).

As the competing nations struggled to establish their North American territories, settlers spread out across the land. Between 1848 and 1859 miners had discovered gold in California and silver in Arizona and Montana, and people began heading west. Native Americans became agitated over the influx of new people—people who built fences—invading the territory that had once been their hunting grounds. And forts were established, such as Fort Larned, to protect the settlers and the trade routes they traveled.

To the west, settlements flourished and faded with a rapidity that could dazzle their inhabitants. Gold rush towns like Bodie, California, sprang up and flourished, attracting thousands of residents, only to wind up as deserted ghost towns a few years later.

And isolated little communities like Fruita, Utah, established to cultivate the land and provide a home to a few people, found that they could hang on to a calm and peaceful existence as long as the sun rose and a little rain fell, and not too many people came through. With the advent of modern highways, Fruita, too, faded into oblivion.

These few settlements are just a sampling of the vast variety of communities and lifestyles that seeded the early days of life on the North American continent—a time when it seemed that in this new land anything was possible if one had the courage, perseverance, and vision to endure. Driven by dreams, whether of wealth, freedom, or peace of mind, these early outposts represent some of the first roots of society to be planted in North American soil. As caretakers today of both that society and soil, may we have the courage, perseverance, and vision to keep not only our dreams but all of our frontiers healthy and alive.

Aztec Ruins National Monument

ANCESTRAL PUEBLO ARCHAEOLOGICAL SITE
Aztec, New Mexico

AT A GLANCE

Built: Beginning ca. A.D. 1108

Considered one of the most significant sites affiliated with the Chaco and Mesa Verde Anasazi, or Ancestral Pueblo cultures

Built in the 12th and 13th centuries, these ruins were excavated beginning in the 19th century and have been carefully preserved and interpreted since 1923. Visitors can walk through a series of rooms with original roofs, constructed beginning about A.D. 1108, and the Great Kiva reconstructed by archaeologist Earl Morris in 1934.

Address:
Aztec Ruins National Monument
P.O. Box 640
84 County Road 2900
Aztec, NM 87410-0640
(505) 334-6174, voice; (505) 334-6372, fax
http://www.nps.gov/azru/

Located between two great centers of prehistoric Native American culture, these ruins represent one of the largest settlements of their era. Built at least two centuries before the peak of the Aztec culture in Mexico, these impressive three-story pueblos were mistakenly named "Aztec Ruins" by early-19th-century Euro-American settlers. Instead, they were home to prehistoric Pueblo Indians known as the Anasazi.

The story of this Place by Flowing Waters is rooted in a larger story that has oriented Pueblo People since the beginning of time. It is the story of Pueblo Emergence, the story of the First People, how they came to be and how they journeyed as a people to "find and be with life."

—*A Trailguide to Aztec Ruins* Southwest Parks and Monuments Association, 1994

♦ ♦ ♦ ♦ ♦

View of Aztec Ruins   (Courtesy of the National Park Service, photo by Fred Mang, Jr.)

The word "Anasazi" comes from a Navajo word that has different meanings, depending on the context and the speaker. It can mean "ancient ones" or "ancient enemies" or "ancient ancestors" or "ancient strangers/enemies." It is the name we have come to use to describe the Native American ancestors who lived in the Southwest. They were the builders of the pueblos of Aztec Ruins and Chaco Canyon. They were the etchers of rock drawings at Petroglyph National Monument near Albuquerque, New Mexico. They were the builders of the massive cliff dwellings at Mesa Verde in southern Colorado, and much more. One encounters the remnants of their homes and buildings all over the Southwest.

About two thousand years ago these originally nomadic people began to live year-round in stationary villages and cultivate crops, and over time they became skillful farmers, architects, artisans, and traders. Living across the broad area we know as Four Corners, their homelands included parts of New Mexico, Arizona, Colorado, and Utah. While archaeologists have found many regional differences in construction methods, architecture styles, and pottery designs, these widely scattered peoples shared similarities in lifestyles that enabled them to flourish despite the rigors of the high desert environment. This settlement known as Aztec Ruins, located in the rich bottomlands of the Animas River and founded around A.D. 1108, is one of the largest pueblo settlements in this area, representing just one part of the long history of life in this region.

Ranging along the north bank of the Animas River near what is now the town of Aztec, New Mexico, these structures were abandoned by their original builders by 1150. Because the style of their construction resembles the style of the Chaco Canyon Anasazi, archaeologists believe that Aztec was probably a Chaco outlier—a sort of suburb—although its large size rivaled the extent of the Chaco Canyon pueblos.

The Aztec pueblos were reoccupied by northern San Juan peoples (from Mesa Verde) during the 1200s, and we see the influence of both the Chaco and Mesa Verde groups in the ruins. The excavated west ruin contains an estimated 405 rooms and 28 kivas (ceremonial rooms), including kivas in the Chacoan and northern San Juan styles, as well as the restored Great Kiva. Some of the rooms are spacious, high-ceilinged Chacoan rooms, and portions of the pueblo were originally three stories high.

Exterior of restored Great Kiva   (Courtesy of the National Park Service, photo by Fred Mang, Jr.)

Later inhabitants reduced the size of some of the large rooms, blocking up older doorways and lowering the ceilings by laying new floors on top of debris with which they had partially filled some of the rooms. They built kivas similar to the ones found in the cliff dwellings of Mesa Verde, and they made changes to the Great Kiva as well.

The huge west pueblo, with its 400 rooms, was the largest of the great houses at Aztec, and several hundred people probably lived there. Massive outer walls contained hundreds of rooms arranged around a central plaza, which had a low row of single-story rooms along one side. Three tiers of rooftops stepped upward to a height of 30 feet on the north wall. The rooms had no doors; cold and wind were kept out by hide coverings or cloth, and for many rooms the only entrance was provided by a hole in the ceiling and a ladder.

In these rooms, mothers prepared food for their children. Grandmothers and grandfathers told stories by firelight to the little ones. Boys and men wove cloth from yucca plant fibers and cotton. They made ceremonial jewelry and chiseled arrows for hunting. Women and girls made pottery and used stones to grind corn into meal.

The structures were built of sandstone, carried in blocks by hand from quarries as much as a mile a way. Beams to support the heavy earthen roofs

The great houses of Aztec, with their multiple levels and carefully constructed walls, were abandoned by 1275. (Courtesy of the National Park Service, photo by Fred Mang, Jr.)

were carried from mountain woodlands as far as 20 miles away. And careful craftsmanship went into the precisely built walls constructed of close-fitting masonry. Many of the walls contained a rubble core, faced with a veneer of stone. And most walls were covered over with an outer layer of plaster that softened the chiseled stone look that the pueblos have today—but also hid the admirable craft that went into their building and design.

Because the pueblos of Aztec went up so quickly, no one is quite sure where the people who built them came from. They may have been nomadic people who were living in the area already and, inspired by their Chacoan neighbors, set to work on building more permanent and secure dwellings. But their expertise with the art of masonry may throw that idea into question. They may instead have emigrated from Chaco Canyon, where architecture and construction were already well-developed, to begin a new settlement in the Animas River valley, where farming was good. Remnants of roadways in the area also echo the vast road system of the Chaco Canyon culture, although archaeologists remain mystified because these roads seem to cut across the land, leading to no particular place, and yet seem to convey a symbolism we have yet to uncover.

But we are sure, judging from the structures they built, that, like their descendants, the Anasazi who built Aztec and lived there were in tune with their surroundings and saw themselves as part of the natural world in which they lived.

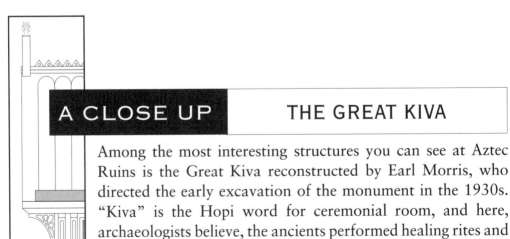

A CLOSE UP   THE GREAT KIVA

Among the most interesting structures you can see at Aztec Ruins is the Great Kiva reconstructed by Earl Morris, who directed the early excavation of the monument in the 1930s. "Kiva" is the Hopi word for ceremonial room, and here, archaeologists believe, the ancients performed healing rites and prayed for rain, luck in hunting, and a bountiful crop. Judging from archaeological evidence and the uses made of the kiva by Pueblo people

Interior view of the Great Kiva showing one of its two entrances (Courtesy of the National Park Service, photo by Fred Mang, Jr.)

A dark red band circles the inside wall above the bench encircling the room. Square openings in the wall let in light. (Courtesy of the National Park Service, photo by Fred Mang, Jr.)

today, the kiva was probably also a community gathering place, used in most of the same ways church buildings are used today.

People entered this great sunken chamber using stairways on the north and south. Its roof was composed of beams and mud, and its shape was a great circle. The Great Kiva reconstruction followed the archaeological evidence uncovered during excavation; in the roof, for example, ponderosa pine beams are crossed by cottonwood poles. Whitewash covers the interior plaster, with a dark red band above the circular bench that runs around the perimeter of the room. Square openings let in light at intervals high on the walls around the room.

In this setting, if one stands very quietly, one can almost imagine the ceremonies that took place here, centuries ago. Here, the People, as their descendants call the earliest ones, celebrated the mystery of life. They sang ancient songs to the beat of their drums. And they danced in the rhythms of the birds and the animals and the natural cycles they knew and felt at one with.

PRESERVING IT FOR THE FUTURE

Aztec Ruins National Monument, New Mexico, was established in 1923 over 320 acres, and excavations have proceeded carefully ever since. But excavation of a ruin strips the protective layers of deposits from its structures and exposes it to damaging weathering processes. Operating under the direction of Earl Morris and the American Museum of Natural History, the conservators allowed time and funds for cleanup and preservation processes before opening sections of the ruins to the public—a new practice at the time.

Reconstruction efforts began in 1933–34, when Morris worked on the Great Kiva, the only such restored structure in existence. Walls of some of the ruins—especially at the Hubbard Tri-Wall Site—have been stabilized by backfilling as a protective measure to keep the walls from crumbling. Several intact roofs also presented special problems, where the weight of the materials and water leakage were causing beams to bend and crack. Finally, most of them were replaced with roofs made of modern materials, which would not cause these problems. Although a great deal of work at Aztec Ruins has been completed, many mounds within the monument still remain unexplored.

In addition to the Visitor Center and museum, the entire West Ruin, with its restored Great Kiva, as well as the Hubbard Tri-Wall Site, are open to the public. The remainder of the monument acreage continues to be researched and protected.

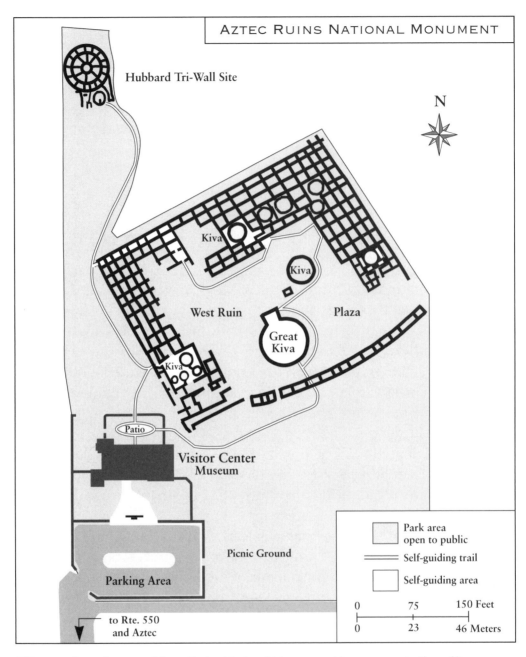

Hubbard Tri-Wall Site

N

Kiva

Kiva

West Ruin

Plaza

Great
Kiva

Kiva

Patio

**Visitor Center
Museum**

Park area
open to public

Self-guiding trail

Self-guiding area

0	75	150 Feet
0	23	46 Meters

Picnic Ground

Parking Area

to Rte. 550
and Aztec

This map shows the areas of Aztec Ruins National Monument that are open to the public. Archaeological excavations in these areas have been completed and steps have been taken to protect structures against further deterioration. Visitors need to take care to minimize the impact of their presence at the site.

EXPLORING ♦ FURTHER

Books about Aztec Ruins, the Anasazi, and Chaco and Mesa Verde Culture

Arnold, Caroline, and Richard Hewitt. *The Ancient Cliff Dwellers of Mesa Verde*. New York: Clarion Books, 1992.

Ayer, Eleanor H. *The Anasazi*. New York: Walker, 1993.

Cordell, Linda S. *Ancient Pueblo Peoples*. Edited by Jeremy A. Sabloff. Washington, D.C.: Smithsonian Books, 1994.

Liptak, Karen. *Indians of the Southwest*. (The First Americans Series) New York: Facts On File, 1991.

Lister, Robert H., and Florence C. Lister. *Aztec Ruins on the Animas: Excavated, Preserved, and Interpreted*. Tucson, Ariz.: Southwest Monuments and Parks Association, 1987.

Mays, Buddy. *Ancient Cities of the Southwest: A Practical Guide to the Major Prehistoric Ruins of Arizona, New Mexico, Utah, and Colorado*. With photographs by Buddy Mays and foreword by Joseph C. Rumberg, Jr. San Francisco: Chronicle Books, 1982.

Peterson, David. *The Anasazi*. A New True Book. Chicago: Childrens Press, 1991.

Warren, Scott. *Cities in the Sand: The Ancient Civilizations of the Southwest*. San Francisco: Chronicle Books, 1992.

Related Places

Chaco Culture National Historical Park
P.O. Box 220
Nageezi, NM 87037
(505) 786-7014

This Anasazi community, located in Chaco Canyon, was probably the largest in the Southwest, with villages scattered up and down the 25-mile canyon, which cuts across the northwestern New Mexico desert. The earliest inhabitants at Aztec Ruins (ca. 1100–50) were probably linked with this culture.

Mesa Verde National Park

Mesa Verde National Park, CO 81330
(970) 529-4465

This National Park includes ancient pit house excavations, cliff dwellings, and pueblo ruins built by the peoples known as the Anasazi. The later group of inhabitants at Aztec Ruins probably came from this area. Visitors to these cool, wooded mesa tops and sheltered side canyons quickly understand what attracted the Ancient Ones to this place as early as A.D. 600. Here, between A.D. 1150 and 1300, during the period now known as the Great Pueblo, the Anasazi built beautiful, massive sandstone structures, nestled into niches in the cliff walls. Of all the cliff dwellings left by the Anasazi, those at Mesa Verde are among the most impressive.

St. Augustine
and Castillo de San Marcos

FIRST PERMANENT EUROPEAN SETTLEMENT AND ITS FORT
St. Augustine, Florida

AT A GLANCE

Built: Town, 1565; the fortress Castillo de San Marcos, 1672–95

Part of the land claim made for the Spanish government by Juan Ponce de
León in 1513; a Spanish fort was first established here in 1565.

Site of the town that grew up around the fort and soon became the seat of
Spanish power in Florida, and the stronghold, Castillo de San Marcos,
that was later erected to protect against pirate raids and encroachment
by the English, who were established at nearby Charleston.

Address:

St. Augustine and St. Johns County
Visitor Information Center
88 Riberia Street, Suite 250
St. Augustine, FL 32084
(800) 653-2489
Visitor and Convention Bureau

Castillo de San Marcos National
Monument Headquarters
One South Castillo Drive
St. Augustine, FL 32084
(904) 829-6506

> *Among the Timucua Indians, the Spanish founded St. Augustine in 1565, after wiping out a French colony perched at the mouth of the St. Johns River. The Spanish colony on Florida's eastern coast became the first European colony to survive, and the city of St. Augustine remains today with hundreds of structures dating back to colonial times, including the great fortress Castillo de San Marcos, which stands today much as it did when it was completed in 1695.*

My personal speculation is that the people of St. Augustine . . . adopted and used a lot of American Indian materials. It may be because they were able to adapt that they survived.

—Anthropologist Kathleen Deagan, 1994

♦ ♦ ♦ ♦ ♦

Aerial view of Castillo de San Marcos   (The St. Johns County Visitors and Convention Bureau)

Controversy swirls around the question of who among the Europeans was the first to arrive in North America. According to a Norse saga, Viking explorers made first contact with North America as early as A.D. 1006, along the northeast coast, and Viking sites have been positively identified along the coast of Newfoundland.

But when we pose the question another way, asking who were the first Europeans to *settle successfully* in North America, the Spanish colony of St. Augustine in Florida—a city that still stands at the mouth of the Matanzas River—wins the prize. When the Italian explorer Christopher Columbus arrived in the New World under the flag of Spain in 1492, all the settlements the Norsemen had established on the North American continent had disappeared. Columbus actually never set foot on the North American continent. That role fell to Spanish explorer Juan Ponce de León, who had sailed with Columbus on his second voyage to the New World (1493–94) and later returned with his own expedition, searching for the fame, fortune, and longevity said to be offered by the legendary "Fountain of Youth." He never found the fountain, but he first sighted the Florida coast on Easter Sunday, March 27, 1513, as he sailed from the coast of Puerto Rico. Believing his new discovery to be another island, he claimed the land for Spain and named it La Florida, meaning "Land of Flowers."

To the Timucua and Calusa Indians who lived along the shores of the Florida peninsula, the arrival of Spanish ships in their waters boded ill. They first heard about the Europeans, no doubt, from their neighbors in the Caribbean islands to the south, after the arrival of Columbus's three ships in 1492. But they soon had their own experiences to draw from. These were a strange and powerful people, with ships that moved like houses on the water, firearms that spit hot metal, and bearded faces. In the years that followed, Spanish slave catchers often came ashore from the great ships to kidnap Indians to sell as slaves to work in mines in the Caribbean Islands. They were aggressive and fierce, and to the Calusas and their neighbors, these strange men were their enemies, come to throw off the balance of their world.

Then, in 1565, a Spanish explorer named Pedro Menéndez de Avilés arrived on the eastern coast with five ships and 600 heavily armed men. This force invaded and captured the Timucuan village of Seloy. Menéndez established a new town on the site of Seloy and called it St. Augustine. The Spanish had come to stay.

St. George Street in St. Augustine: Interpreters portray daily life in the 18th century.
(The St. Johns County Visitors and Convention Bureau)

English settlers—often thought of as the first to arrive—did not establish their first successful community, at Jamestown in what is now Virginia, for another 42 years. (The earlier Roanoke colony was abandoned after only two years.) And the Pilgrims' famous 1620 landing to the north, at Plymouth Rock, was a full 55 years in the future.

However, Spain did face a challenge in Florida. France had established Fort Caroline, a colony protected by a small fort on Florida's St. Johns River. Although the Spanish had sent several expeditions against Fort Caroline, they could not take it, and Spain feared that the French would establish dominance in the area. Given orders by King Philip II of Spain to establish a settlement and drive off or kill any "pirates" or settlers from other nations, Menéndez immediately launched a new assault on the French settlement. He and his men destroyed Fort Caroline completely, slaughtering all its male inhabitants. With that mission completed, he turned to building up and expanding St. Augustine.

Today, St. Augustine provides a fascinating journey through nearly 500 years of history. The streets are laid out in the distinctive plan typical of 16th-century Spanish colonial walled towns, and many of the picturesque buildings date from the colonial period, 1703–1821. Horse-drawn carriages roll lazily past the old Spanish houses adorned with wrought-iron grilles and balconies. With over 144 blocks of historic houses listed on the National Register of Historic Places, living history museums, and hundreds of actors strolling the streets in period costumes (their roles range from colonial craftsmen to British fusiliers), the city is a living time capsule reflecting its many years of continuous survival.

No small part of that survival is the imposing fortress Castillo de San Marcos, located just outside the city gates. The oldest masonry fortification in the continental United States, the fort was built by the Spanish over a 23-year period between 1672 and 1695. It was designed to protect against English attacks on the town of St. Augustine and on the galleons sailing to Spain with cargoes of gold from Mexico. Surviving two major sieges in 1702 and 1740, as well as numerous Indian attacks, Castillo de San Marcos was

Front of fort, showing moat and tower   (The St. Johns County Visitors and Convention Bureau)

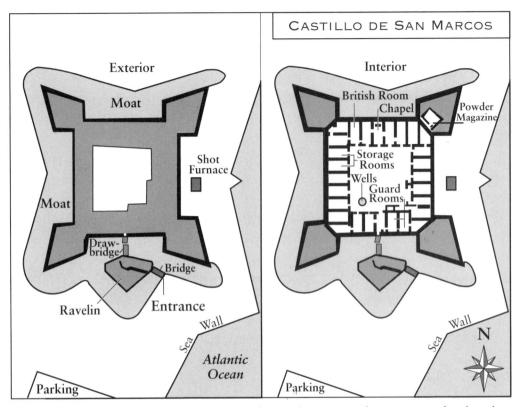

Visitors to the Castillo de San Marcos can tour the guard rooms, powder magazine, chapel, and storage rooms, as well as the upper level where Spanish soldiers once stood watch and fired cannon to protect the settlement. One room on the lower level has also been set aside to commemorate the British period at the fort.

never captured by an enemy in battle. Today, still poised on the threshold of the city like a vigilant watchdog, Castillo de San Marcos remains a formidable edifice.

Originally surrounded completely by a moat 1,509 feet in circumference, Castillo de San Marcos was designed with only a solitary opening for entrance and exit. Built in the shape of a large hollow square with diamond-shaped bastions at each corner, its walls tower 33 feet above the original moat floor. Even today, it is completely commanding in its suggestion of sheer strength.

As you enter the fort through the ravelin, a triangular outerwork shielding the entrance, you cross two reconstructed drawbridges—a small bridge at the entrance to the ravelin and a main drawbridge at the entrance to the fort itself. In its working days, the ravelin drawbridge was raised each night at sunset to secure the fort, while the larger drawbridge needed to be raised only when the fort was under attack. Once inside, a glance around the Castillo de San Marcos quickly reveals why the fort was never lost in battle. Built of coquina stone (a shell sandstone quarried nearby), the north, south, and west walls are 9 feet thick at the top and 14 feet thick at the base. Even more heavily reinforced, the east wall measures 11 feet thick at the top and 19 feet at the base. The four bastions—composed of solid fill combining sand, stone, and trash—are built to support the heavy cannons that once inflicted a deadly crossfire on approaching attackers. Buried deep inside the fill of one of the bastions is the original powder magazine. Here, within thick walls additionally protected by the surrounding earth and fill, soldiers originally stored their gunpowder safely away from the enemy's oncoming shot. Eventually the dampness caused by the room's total lack of ventilation threatened to ruin the gunpowder, so it was stored at various other locations throughout the years, and the magazine was then adapted to a variety of other uses.

Moving around at random inside of the fort, visitors can see much of its original layout as designed by the Spanish engineer Ignacio Daza. Nearest the entrance are the guardrooms. Since St. Augustine was a garrison town, or *presidio*, the fort's soldiers lived in town with their families and came to the fort only on their rounds of duty, usually 24-hour shifts. The guardrooms were set up to accommodate the soldiers, much like the living quarters in firehouses today are set up to accommodate the firefighters on duty. Platforms that are still attached to the walls served as bunks for sleeping, and large fireplaces kept soldiers warm on cold days as well as providing the fire to cook their meals. Three shallow wells, one of which can still be seen in the central plaza, provided water.

A long bank of storage rooms, which at first glance look like prison cells, can be seen on the left side of the central plaza from the entrance, as you face the fort's interior. These rooms would usually be crammed full of everything that the fort needed, from ammunition and weapons to lumber, tools, and provisions such as dried beans, flour, rice, and corn. The stockpiles of food and ammunition were important not only to the fort but also to the entire town of St. Augustine in the event of a siege.

Equally important to the soldiers was the chapel, located directly across the central plaza from the entrance. A major part of daily Spanish life, the chapel was used by the fort's inhabitants for prayer and Mass. With the introduction of Christianity to the Indians around Fort Augustine, the Spanish mission system became established more than 100 years before its introduction to what is now Texas or on the continent's West Coast.

Located between the chapel and the storage rooms is the British Room, which interprets a brief though important period between 1763 and 1784, when British troops occupied the fort after Spain peacefully ceded Florida to Great Britain in exchange for the fortified harbor and city of La Habaña, Cuba. The British vacated the fort when Florida was returned to Spanish rule after the end of the American Revolution in 1783.

Not surprisingly, the so-called British Period had a great impact on St. Augustine and Castillo de San Marcos. During this time the Spanish settlers left Florida in a mass exodus, and St. Augustine lost most of its population and portable wealth. With the influx of English troops and families, as well as a new group of colonists (now known as Minorcans) from the Mediterranean islands, the character of the town and fort, once strictly Spanish,

Interpreters dressed as soldiers prepare cannon for firing.   (The St. Johns County Visitors and Convention Bureau)

became more multicultural and multinational. With the return of Spanish control in 1784 there was some attempt to revive the old ways, but too much had changed. St. Augustine still "looked" Spanish, but its exclusively Spanish and Catholic way of life had been forever altered, making room for a wider range of cultural and social expression.

Finally, in 1819, with the Spanish empire in the New World crumbling throughout Central and South America as well as Mexico, Spain relinquished Florida, turning it over to the United States. The City of St. Augustine was already 256 years old when United States representatives officially took possession of the province of East Florida. On July 10, 1821, the Spanish flag was lowered from atop the Castillo de San Marcos, and in its place rose the Stars and Stripes.

In the 1840s the U.S. Army filled the east side of the moat and mounted seacoast artillery pieces along the seawall. The shot furnace, located within this wall and just outside the fort, was used to heat cannonballs, the idea being to set an attacker's wooden ships on fire. The furnace that produced this "hot shot" can still be seen today.

As a protector of the area, the Castillo served St. Augustine well. Under Spanish rule, the fort successfully withstood two brutal, major sieges. The first, in 1702, lasted 50 days, and the second, in 1740, lasted 28 days. Although Castillo de San Marcos changed hands several times, it was never defeated in battle. Twice the Spanish relinquished it by treaty—to the British in exchange for Cuba's capital in 1763 (regained by treaty in 1783) and to the United States in 1821.

Under American rule, the venerable Castillo became Fort Marion and saw duty as a penal colony for detaining Indian prisoners during the Seminole Wars and later for imprisoning Indians captured between 1875 and 1878 in western military campaigns. During the Civil War, Florida joined the Confederacy, and Confederate soldiers held Fort Marion briefly, but the Union Army soon overtook the area and, with it, the fort. In 1942, after the fort became a National Monument, the original Spanish name was restored.

Visitors to St. Augustine and Castillo de San Marcos today are reminded of the diverse multiculturalism that shaped America's early history and of the rich traditions imbedded not only in our past, but in our present.

A CLOSE UP — REMNANTS OF THE FIRST FORT

In 1994 archaeologists made an exciting discovery on the grounds of an old Spanish Mission in St. Augustine. Nine inches below the surface of the grounds of the Nombre de Dios Mission, they discovered the remains of an ancient triangular moat, burned timbers and bits of pottery, spikes and old musket shot. On investigation, they concluded these were most likely part of an early small fort erected by Pedro Menéndez de Avilés to protect the original St. Augustine colony. Among the discoveries at the site were bits of charred wheat. "This was our first clue that this was definitely a post-Spanish-arrival site," said anthropologist Kathleen Deagan. "There was no wheat in America before the Europeans came. . . . It's an exciting discovery for us because it's really the earliest European site within the first European town in the United States." After testing the other materials, researchers were confident that the finds belonged to the period of the city's founding.

Researchers hope that their discovery may also give some clues as to why St. Augustine managed to survive in its earliest days when other fledgling colonies such as the one at Roanoke, Virginia, failed.

"My personal speculation is that the people of St. Augustine . . . adopted and used a lot of American Indian materials," Deagan announced. "It may be because they were able to adapt that they survived."

PRESERVING IT FOR THE FUTURE

Castillo de San Marcos is the oldest masonry fortification in the continental United States. It is the only 17th-century fort still standing intact in the United States and is one of the finest and purest examples of Spanish military

Tower of Castillo de San Marcos (The St. Johns County Visitors and Convention Bureau)

architecture from this period left in the world. It survived two major sieges and it served 228 continuous years as a commissioned military base (1672–1900). Since that time, the structure has continued as a government-owned site and continues to serve the public as a historical monument.

The historic structures within the city have their own stories, and preservation of the cultural and historic heritage of St. Augustine has long been important here. The National Register of Historic Places has helped in the preservation of the legacy left by the earliest Spanish colonists, by those who followed during the English period, and finally by the Americans who took possession of the city in the 19th century.

EXPLORING ♦ FURTHER

Books about St. Augustine and the Spanish Presence in Florida

Arana, Luis R., and Albert Manucy. *The Building of Castillo de San Marcos.* [St. Augustine, Fla.]: Eastern National Park & Monument Association for Castillo de San Marcos National Monument, 1977.

Manucy, Albert C. *The Houses of St. Augustine, 1565–1821.* (A Florida Sand Dollar Book) Gainesville: University Press of Florida, 1992.

Matter, Robert Allen. *Pre-Seminole Florida: Spanish Soldiers, Friars, and Indian Missions, 1513–1763.* New York: Garland Publishing, 1990.

Related Place

Fort Matanzas National Monument
8635 A1A South
St. Augustine, FL 32086
(904) 471-0116
Located 14 miles south of St. Augustine,
reached via Florida A1A on Anastasia Island

The beaches where Fort Matanzas stands were the scene of slaughters (*matanza* means "slaughter" in Spanish), in which between 200 and 300 Frenchmen met their death on September 29 and October 12, 1565, at the hands of Spanish soldiers from St. Augustine. The site was also St. Augustine's only vulnerable approach: if attackers could cross the inlet bar here they could travel up the Matanzas or San Sebastian Rivers and launch a surprise attack. Built in 1742, Fort Matanzas helped fortify the strategic Spanish position on the Florida coast, adding to the formidable protection offered by the Castillo de San Marcos. Visitors use a ferry to reach the fort, which is located on Rattlesnake Island.

Colonial Pemaquid

A VILLAGE FROZEN IN TIME
Bristol, Maine

AT A GLANCE

Built: First settlement, 1610; Fort Charles, 1677; Fort William Henry, 1692; Fort Frederick, 1729–31

Site of early European settlements dating back to 1610, protected by a series of forts.

Located on a point of land at the mouth of the Pemaquid River in Bristol, this site welcomed fishing and trading ships as early as 1610, with as many as 109 ships dropping anchor between 1607 and 1622. During this time, and long before, Pemaquid Indians (an Abnaki/Algonquian tribe) lived and fished in this area, as did even earlier Native Americans.

Address:
Colonial Pemaquid
Bristol, ME 04539
Summer season (207) 677-2433
Off-season (207) 624-6080
Four miles from Damariscotta on Maine Route 129,
then Maine Route 130 for nine miles, bear right one mile

> Situated on a point of land at the mouth of the Pemaquid River in Bristol, Maine,
> Colonial Pemaquid State Park preserves the remains of three forts and some
> 14 foundations of 17th- and 18th-century structures, as well as the officers'
> quarters of two forts that once protected this peninsula: Fort William Henry
> and Fort Frederick. (The first, Fort Charles, remains unexcavated.)

There have been for a long time seven or eight considerable
Dwellings about Pemmaquid, which is well accomodated
with Pasture Land about the Haven for feeding Cattel, and
some Fields also for Tillage.

—William Hubbard (1621?–1704),
*The History of the Indian Wars
in New England . . . to 1677*

♦ ♦ ♦ ♦ ♦

Despite this rather glowing report, a stormy saga surrounds the little strip of land that juts out into the Pemaquid River at Bristol. Three different times, English settlers tried to build forts here to protect the inland areas. And three times they failed.

Aerial view of Pemaquid   (Colonial Pemaquid State Historic Site, Bristol, Maine, photo by Nicholas Dean)

Standing on this peninsula, looking out over the harbor it protects, it's easy to imagine some of the feelings of amazement and fear that must have risen in the Abnaki and Micmac Indians as they sighted the huge sailing ships that hovered on the ocean horizon and then bore down upon the cozy cove. The first Europeans weighed anchor here as early as 1607 and may have established a temporary settlement in 1610. The newcomers were mostly fishermen and fur traders working the coast; they came to value the shelter provided by the harbor at the mouth of the Pemaquid River, whose name comes from the Abnaki language. We don't know much about the life of the Native Americans who lived here prior to that, although they were here long before the Europeans arrived in Pemaquid. They often camped on the peninsula and buried some of their dead here.

By the mid-1620s, after the Pilgrims landed at Plymouth Rock to the South, English settlers began arriving in Pemaquid. The land was tillable, and so they farmed. But the prime seacoast and harbor location made this an ideal spot for trading and fishing as well. They traded often with the Massachusetts Bay Colony as well as with the Abnaki and Micmac. Life along the Maine coast was less harsh in the winter than it was farther inland, and the spot seemed favorable for a growing town.

By the 1670s as many as 200 people may have made the Pemaquid area their home. But, unfortunately, this otherwise healthy settlement site was destined to get caught up in political shifts, wars, and instability that would prevent the little pioneer community from thriving. For many years the most northeastern English community in the New World, Pemaquid became the first line of defense for English colonialism against attacks from the French to the north. Both factions claimed the site, and Pemaquid was caught in the squeeze.

The first devastation came in 1676 when the Abnaki Indians burned the village during an uprising of native peoples throughout New England. This was the first signal to the community that they needed protection, and the following year, they constructed Fort Charles, the first of three fortifications to be built there. But Fort Charles was no help.

Fearful that increasing numbers of English settlers in the region threatened their way of life, the Abnaki—like other Indians in the region—readily allied themselves with the French, who encouraged both their suspicions and their aggressiveness.

The reconstructed bastion, or great tower, of Fort William Henry   (Colonial Pemaquid State Historic Site, Bristol, Maine, photo courtesy of Maine Historic Preservation Commission)

In 1689 both fort and village came under attack again from the Abnaki. Although the fort initially held, it finally succumbed to fire directed from a huge bedrock formation just to the west. (Later fort builders extended the fortifications to enclose this site.) The losses were heavy. A French missionary known only as Thury accompanied the Abnaki (French soldiers stayed away, shrewdly leaving the Indians to take all the blame), and he gave a particularly chilling account of the assault by the enraged warriors: "They put to flight all those in their nightclothes and threw themselves in their manner on the houses breaking down the doors, taking and killing all whom they found inside." Pemaquid was demolished and its citizens routed once again.

Recognizing the strategic importance of this northern outpost, the Massachusetts Bay Colony erected another, stronger fort three years later, in 1692. As you visit the site today, you can identify the area once occupied by Fort William Henry, defined by low stone walls that mark out a large rectangular shape and a tall stone tower, or bastion (which was reconstructed in 1908).

Massachusetts Governor Sir William Phips placed great hopes in this fort, spending £20,000—two-thirds of the colony's entire budget—on protecting the outpost. Workers hauled 2,000 cartloads of stone to the site to build walls 10 to 22 feet high, plus the stone bastion, which towered 29 feet high. A garrison of 60 men, armed with 20 cannon, were stationed here, and 28 gun ports lined the outer wall. It was impressive. "I have caused a large stone fort, called Fort William Henry, to be built at Pemaquid," wrote the governor in 1693. "The fort is strong enough to resist all the Indians in America."

But he was wrong.

Early in August 1696, three French warships, along with about 100 French soldiers and some 500 Indians, descended upon Fort William Henry. The fort

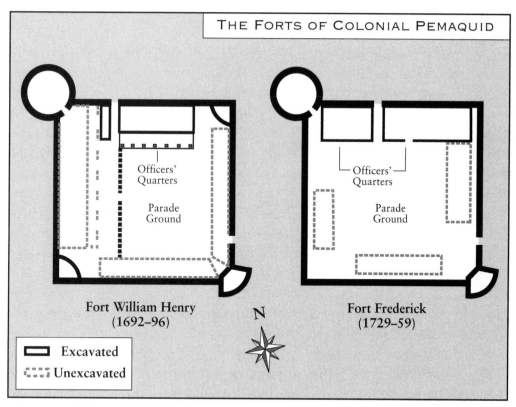

The outlines of these structures are shown as archaeologists believe they looked. Fort Frederick was built on top of the ruins of Fort William Henry.

that seemed so strong could not withstand this assault. The mortar used in building the stone walls, it turned out, was of such inferior quality that the interior buildings were shaken to their foundations by the attackers' cannon. Furthermore, the garrison's water supply was outside the walls of the fort—a severe tactical error. With his garrison vastly outnumbered, the commander of the fort, Captain Pascho Chubb, surrendered. "The fort being completely demolished to the base of the foundations," wrote French commander Pierre Le Moyne, Sieur d'Iberville, "we all set sail."

After the destruction of 1696, Pemaquid lay abandoned for 35 years, until Colonel David Dunbar set out to resettle the area. Beginning in 1729, work began on a new structure, Fort Frederick, built on the old fort's foundations. Dunbar brought 200 Scotch-Irish settlers from Boston to the little peninsula. They cleared land, laid out streets, and raised frames for 30 to 40 houses. Several of the foundations that you can still see today date back to this period. A natural leader, Dunbar appeared to be shaping a thriving community that exuded both energy and promise.

Two years later, a man named Robert Hale visited Pemaquid and wrote this glowing description of Dunbar and the town in his journal: "He's a very Free, Affable, Courteous Gentleman, very personable & tall, about 40 Years of Age. Here are now 5 Sloops & 2 Schooners in ye Harbour. The Town is Call'd Frederick's Fort. The House Lots of which more than 100 are but about 30 feet wide and 100 feet long, about 8 houses are up and about 15 frames more in ye Town."

But the project had a short life, snuffed out when conflicting land claims forced Dunbar to leave Pemaquid in 1731. When he left, the driving force he had provided left with him. The community began to disperse, and soon no one was left. Massachusetts Bay Colony did send a garrison to Fort Frederick from 1732 to 1759, but as the French and Indian Wars finally came to an end, so too did life at Pemaquid. Unlike most New England towns, this little community had shown its greatest strength in the 1600s, not in the years leading up to and following the American Revolution.

But this strange fact has left us with a rare gift: A 17th-century village, with its forts, frozen in time and left untouched until the late 19th and mid-20th century. Only then did archaeologists begin to bring their scientific expertise to the questions raised by its many remains—partially hidden beneath layers of dirt and nearly three centuries of weathering.

Excavations at Fort William Henry and Fort Frederick   (Colonial Pemaquid State Historic Site, Bristol, Maine, photo courtesy of Maine Historic Preservation Commission)

Writing before Dunbar made his last valiant attempt at settling the Pemaquid peninsula, Colonel Wolfgang William Romer, a British military engineer, perhaps best summed up the fate of Pemaquid when he wrote in 1699:

> The land of Pemaquid is much better than that about St. George's [a neighboring village]. There was there formerly a village of 36 well built houses on a neck of land, where stood the fort, and there were many farms and farmers in the neighboring country. 'Tis supposed that had peace continued Pemaquid would have been a place of importance because of its fishery, its trade with the Indians and the trade which would have arisen from the productions of the country.

But it was not to be. Instead, Pemaquid is a mysterious and intriguing group of stones and artifacts emerging from the earth to tell us stories about a past that we could only guess at before archaeologists began their digging.

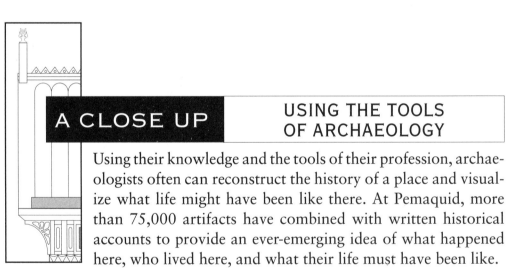

A CLOSE UP — USING THE TOOLS OF ARCHAEOLOGY

Using their knowledge and the tools of their profession, archaeologists often can reconstruct the history of a place and visualize what life might have been like there. At Pemaquid, more than 75,000 artifacts have combined with written historical accounts to provide an ever-emerging idea of what happened here, who lived here, and what their life must have been like.

For example, among the remains uncovered by archaeologists at the Pemaquid settlement site, they found an interesting group of artifacts around the foundation of one large building that have led them to an educated guess: This building may well have been among those destroyed in one of the early Abnaki attacks on the village. Burned planks and timbers unearthed here bespeak the dangers and uncertainties of the life led by these settlers along

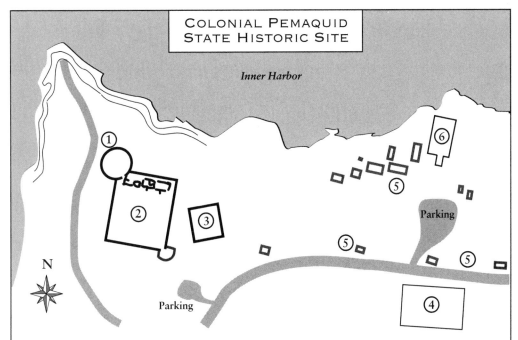

COLONIAL PEMAQUID
STATE HISTORIC SITE

Inner Harbor

Parking

N

Parking

1 The reconstructed great western tower of Fort William Henry (1692–96). Open to the public, this structure contains artifacts from the excavations at Pemaquid

2 Excavated remains of the walls and structures of Fort William Henry, as well as the vestiges of Fort Frederick (1729–59), which was built on the ruins of the earlier stronghold

3 House built c. 1800, which now serves as a research center for archaeologists

4 Cemetery, the central burial ground for the Pemaquid settlement

5 The excavated foundations of early Pemaquid's buildings. Interpretive signs show graphic representations of what archaeologists think the houses looked like

6 The Colonial Pemaquid Museum, displaying and interpreting many of the European and Native American artifacts recovered during archaeological excavations

the Maine coast. Numerous bricks found inside the structure's north wall indicate that the building's chimney toppled as it burned. And, while the fire could have been accidental, it also may well have been set during the destruction of the village in 1676 or 1689.

Archaeologists can also see that the house was sturdily built—framed with hewn timbers, which were sheathed with sawn boards and then covered with hand-split clapboards or shingles, providing a measure of insulation against the bitterly cold New England winters. The Abnaki were right in thinking that the English settlers had come to stay.

Also, unlike English farmhouses, where cellars were uncommon and food was kept in above-ground storage areas, this house appears to have had a cellar. The settlers had quickly realized that cellars provided a way to keep food cool but not frozen in sub-zero temperatures. And they had designed cellars into their houses.

From the cellar area of this house, researchers unearthed redware and stoneware jars once used for storing food. Among the rubble they also found a silver thimble, a Massachusetts Pine Tree sixpence silver coin, and two stamps—one silver and one brass—for sealing letters with wax. Though meager, these small indications of a lifestyle provide a powerful link to the family that once lived here, writing and sealing letters, mending clothes, storing food, and taking stock of their finances.

PRESERVING IT FOR THE FUTURE

The settlement at Pemaquid and its succession of forts lay forgotten for nearly 150 years, until antiquarian John Henry Cartland set about excavating it in the late 19th century. His findings at Fort William Henry, Fort Frederick, and the Pemaquid settlement piqued local interest, and in 1902 the State of Maine was given the fort site. By 1908 the state had reconstructed the great western tower of Fort William Henry. In 1923, while looking on the peninsula, without success, for traces of a conjectured Viking settlement, archaeologist Warren King Moorehead exposed additional portions of both the fort and the village.

But not until 1965 did modern archaeological investigations begin, led by Helen Camp (whose book you'll find listed under "Exploring Further"). She began in earnest to search for Pemaquid's 17th- and 18th-century village. Because of the significance of the remains she uncovered, the Maine Bureau of Parks and Recreation acquired the property in 1969. Up to the mid-1970s, Helen Camp and Robert Bradley codirected the excavations and research begun by Camp, uncovering the officers' quarters and other features of both Fort William Henry and Fort Frederick.

Archaeologists have unearthed a wealth of information about the life of this small community that existed on the northern New England frontier for more than a century. The archaelogical site was proclaimed a National Historic Landmark in 1993.

Visitors can explore the museum inside the reconstructed Fort William Henry tower, where many of the uncovered artifacts are on display, including 17th- and 18th-century musket balls, coins, pottery, and early hardware. Park rangers offer guided tours of the archaeological digs during the summer months, and visitors can also use the interpretive signs to take a self-guided tour.

EXPLORING ♦ FURTHER

Books about Pemaquid, Its Forts, and Other Settlements in Maine

Bradley, Robert L. *The Forts of Maine, 1607–1945: An Archaeological and Historical Survey.* [Augusta]: Maine Historic Preservation Commission, Maine Bureau of Parks and Recreation, 1981.

Brebner, John B. *New England's Outpost: Acadia Before the Conquest of Canada.* New York: Burt Franklin, 1973.

Camp, Helen B. *Archaeological Excavations at Pemaquid, Maine, 1965–1974.* Augusta: Maine State Museum, 1976.

Ochoa, George. *The Fall of Quebec and the French and Indian War.* (Turning Points in American History) New York: Silver Burdett, 1991.

Radlauer, Ruth Shaw. *Acadia National Park.* Chicago: Childrens Press, 1978.

Rich, Louise Dickinson. *The Coast of Maine: An Informal History and Guide.* Photographs by Samuel Chamberlain. Camden, Me.: Down East Books, 1993.

Related Place

Fishermen's Museum
Pemaquid Point Lighthouse
Rt. 130
Pemaquid, ME 04558
(207) 677-2726 or 2494

Located on the west side of the entrance to Muscongus Bay in Maine, the first lighthouse on this point was built during the period 1824–27. The original stone structure was rebuilt in 1835, with the addition in 1897 of a redbrick structure to house an automatic bell-striking machine. The lighthouse is still operational today. In 1934 it was automated and deeded to the town of Bristol. The entire site is now known as Pemaquid Point Lighthouse Park and includes the Fishermen's Museum, located in the former lighthouse keeper's house. At the museum, visitors can see artifacts connected with Maine's fishing industry and, outside, they can experience the crashing surf against the rocks, spectacular sunrises, and dense, rolling fog that were all part of everyday life for the lighthouse keepers who once lived here.

San Antonio Missions National Historic Park

A MEETING OF TWO CULTURES
San Antonio, Texas

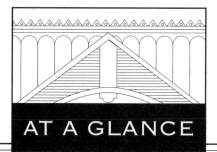

AT A GLANCE

Built: Beginning in 1690

Four Spanish missions, stretched out along the nine-mile-long "Mission Trail" in San Antonio.

This National Historic Park preserves four Spanish missions, which played an integral part in the Spanish colonization system that stretched across the Southwest and into California in the 17th, 18th, and 19th centuries. The park's structures include Mission San José, San Juan, Espada, and Concepción.

Address:
Headquarters: San Antonio Missions National Historic Park
2202 Roosevelt Avenue
San Antonio, TX 78210
(210) 534-8833, Headquarters
(210) 932-1001, Visitors' Center

Over 400 years ago, Spanish expeditions began to explore land that is now the American Southwest. Beginning in the 16th century, missionaries accompanied by a few soldiers moved north out of the Valley of Mexico, founding missions and presidios (forts). By 1718 this activity extended to the San Antonio River, helping to form the nucleus of the future city of San Antonio. Here two vastly different peoples met, as the missionaries sought to teach the culture of Spanish Catholicism to hunter-gatherer Coahuiltecan Indians who lived nearby.

Grant me the treasure of sublime poverty: permit the distinctive sign of our order to be that it does not possess anything of its own beneath the sun, for the glory of your name, and that it have no other patrimony than begging.
—St. Francis of Assisi (ca. 1182–1226), founder of the Franciscan Order

♦ ♦ ♦ ♦ ♦

Church, Mission San José (Mission San José y San Miguel de Aguayo) (Courtesy of the National Park Service)

Stretched out along the nine-mile Mission Trail in San Antonio, Texas, the four beautiful, old Spanish missions that comprise the San Antonio Missions National Historic Park are a part of a mission system that stretched across the Spanish Southwest in the 17th, 18th, and 19th centuries. Mission San José, Mission Concepción, Mission San Juan, and Mission Espada—there is something quietly romantic in the names, giving rise to images of gentle and serene friars in frocks and sandals moving down brightly sunlit and dusty roads, kindly administering their duties.

You can imagine the friars tending the poor, giving consolation, food, drink, words of wisdom, and religious instruction to their flocks. You can hear the mission bells tolling their call for evening services and the beating wings of swallows as they dart from rooftop to rooftop—even, perhaps, the quiet faraway sound of a Spanish guitar playing gently in the moonlight.

There is much in this picture that rings true. But the whole story of the missions is much more complex than such simple images convey.

Religion and charity were not the sole functions of these beautiful old Spanish missions. For Spain, in those early centuries, the establishment of missions was a major part of a plan to develop and manage a colonial frontier in what is now the American Southwest.

With few soldiers or settlers at their disposal, the Spanish had a problem if they wanted to keep the vast Southwest out of the hands of other nations—particularly the French, who in the late 17th century had begun to make inroads into the Southwest from Louisiana. Spain's strategy was to use one of its strongest allies, the Catholic Church, to help hold and protect the land.

In Spain, Catholicism was at the very heart of the nation's culture. Church and state were closely and intricately linked, with the church acting as the arm of the state as often as the state acted as the arm of the church. By "permitting" the church to establish missions in the New World, the state was trying to ensure that Native peoples would be converted not only to Catholicism but also to Spain and the Spanish way of life. The missions would function like the feudal estates of medieval Europe, with the work being done by "peasants" who remained loyal to both church and state. The chain of missions established along the San Antonio River in the 18th century are reminders of how successful the Spanish strategy was.

In 1690, Spain began establishing missions in what is now East Texas; in addition, a small way-station for travelers was built in 1718 in a cottonwood grove along the banks of the San Antonio River. Although it was the first to be completed, this mission, named San Antonio de Valero, failed after only a short period. However, it found everlasting fame in 1836, when, having been converted into a fort and renamed the Alamo, it became the site of one of the most legendary battles in American history.

Although San Antonio de Valero failed to sustain itself, Fray Antonio Margil de Jesús, taking note of a large population of Coahuiltecan Indians in the San Antonio River area, established Mission San José (San José y San Miguel de Aguayo) on the east bank of the river in 1720. It was relocated to the west bank sometime before 1727.

Coahuiltecan is actually a name that historians have given to a number of hunter-gatherer groups of Indians who lived in an area extending southward from San Antonio de Rio to the Rio Grande. Although these bands had different dialects and religious beliefs, they also had much in common. They were nomads who lived off the arid cactus and brush country, and their basic social units were extended families, which joined to form larger bands when food was abundant. Although good times might find the Coahuiltecan hunting down deer or wild pigs and fishing with bow and arrows, more often than not they subsisted on the nourishment provided by the land. Their principal foods were vegetables, roots, nuts, and tunas (the fruit of the prickly pear cactus), but when times were hard they also ate rodents, insects, lizards, and snakes. Tattooed in the styles of their particular bands, they wore breechcloths or hide skirts, fiber sandals, and, in bad weather, cloaks made from animal hides. Their shelters were sparse, usually small temporary huts fashioned from brushwood and grass. Not by nature fierce warriors, they were often forced to band together to protect themselves from raids by the Lipan Apache and Comanche, who also inhabited the area.

Given the difficult struggle for existence faced daily by the Coahuiltecan, it isn't surprising that this people was attracted by the regular food and shelter the mission offered. They were recruited without too much difficulty. Recruitment generally meant that, in exchange for food and shelter, they subjected their bodies to hard labor and submitted their minds to religious instruction and conversion.

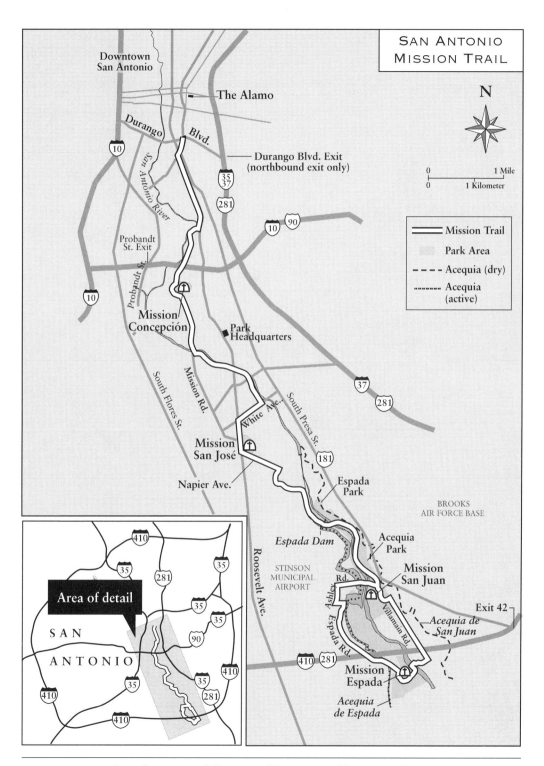

Encouraged and aided by the Franciscans, the Coahuiltecan soon constructed their own settlements around the walls of the mission complex. They were used to hard labor, and, under the guidance of the Franciscans who directed the missions, their conversions put them in the hands of a basically humanitarian and enlightened order—since the Franciscans preferred practical application of belief to stern and rigid doctrine.

Still, the object of the missions was to indoctrinate the converts in the ideas and acceptance of the church and to make them loyal supporters of Spain, as well. An assessment of the missions' value and history wouldn't be complete without taking into account this basically exploitative function. The converts' days were strictly structured around work and the required religious rituals, with little time left over to think about the changes in their existence. Once independent and nomadic, they were organized into small, closely regulated medieval-type villages, with the parent mission, representing both God and Spain, acting as feudal lord. As a result, much of the Coahuiltecan culture and natural way of life was lost over the years.

The Rose Window at Mission San José demonstrates the fine craftsmanship of artisans who worked on the missions. (Courtesy of the National Park Service)

On the other hand, the culture of the United States has gained much, thanks to the establishment of the missions and the rich mixture of Spanish and Indian heritage handed down to us.

With the established base of the Coahuiltecan, as well as an abundant supply of water and timber from the rich San Antonio River valley, Mission San José was a success from the beginning. And when the less well situated East Texas missions began to fail from drought, disease, and French incursion, three of those declining missions

Church and Convento, Mission Concepción (*Mission Nuestra Señora de la Purísima Concepción de Acuña*)   (Courtesy of the National Park Service)

—Concepción, San Juan, and Espada—were relocated to spots near the more successful San José in the San Antonio valley. Here, grouped together, protected by a small presidio and mutually supportive, they, too, quickly prospered, and the missions and the Indian settlements around them became the seeds for one of the most successful Spanish communities in Texas, a community that would eventually become the thriving city of San Antonio.

Known as the Queen of the Missions, Mission San José remained throughout its history the largest and most prosperous in the San Antonio area. During its peak years, its community numbered around 300 Indians sustained by extensive agricultural fields and large herds of livestock. An imposing complex of stone walls, bastions, a granary, and a magnificent church, the mission also quickly gained a reputation as a social and cultural center. Not surprisingly it also became a target of raids by decidedly unconverted Apache and Comanche Indians. Some quick lessons given by Spanish soldiers from the nearby presidio helped the mission Indians learn how to handle guns as well as their bows and arrows, and their talent with the new weapons, combined with the thick outer walls, made Mission San José nearly impregnable. A visiting friar, Juan Agustín Morfi, attested to the mission's defensive character when he wrote, "It is in truth, the first mission in America . . . in point of beauty, plan, and strength . . . there is not a presidio along the entire frontier that can compare with it."

Time, though, managed to do what raiding Indians could not. After the Mission San José was secularized along with the other San Antonio missions in 1824, the mission turned its lands over to local Indians, and its church was left to the supervision of a local parish priest. In the years that followed, the Mission San José complex fell victim to neglect and decay. Its north wall collapsed in a storm in 1868, and its dome and roof fell in another storm on Christmas Day, 1873. Today, however, with the compound restored to its original appearance, including reconstructed walls and Indian dwellings,

Façade and Espadaña (bell tower) of the church, Mission Espada (Mission San Francisco de la Espada) (Courtesy of the National Park Service)

Mission San José still retains its original façade. The church still functions as an active parish, as do the nearby Missions Concepción, San Juan, and Espada.

Of the four, Mission Concepción, distinguished by a massive church with twin towers and cupola, retains the largest proportion of original structures. It is the oldest unrestored stone church in the United States. Missions San Juan and Espada, like Mission San José, have been restored to a close approximation of their original appearance.

A favorite of many students of the Spanish period in the United States as well as amateur and professional photographers, Mission Espada features a colorful weathered appearance and an unusual broken-arch doorway. Its *acequia*, or aqueduct, system, still supplies water as in the past to the mission and surrounding lands.

Mission San Juan, with its small chapel and open bell tower, houses a restored missionary residence, artifacts of the Spanish period, and the ruins of a larger uncompleted church.

Taken together, the 250- to 300-year-old structures along San Antonio's Mission Trail offer a rich and virtually unbroken connection to the Spanish heritage of the great Southwest.

A CLOSE UP — THE ACEQUIA OF MISSION ESPADA

Self-sufficiency was a key to the mission system, and water was essential to success. Only with water could crops be planted, grown, and harvested. Challenged by the sparse rainfall of the arid Texas climate, the Franciscans made irrigation a high priority. In fact, irrigation in Spanish Texas was so important that cropland was measured in *suertes*, the amount of land that could be watered in one day.

The Spanish Franciscans had learned how to use *acequias*, or irrigation ditches, from the Muslims, who came from a land as arid as Texas and had introduced their use in Spain. Along the San Antonio River, missionaries and Indians built a system of seven gravity-flow ditches, augmented by five dams and an aqueduct, creating a 15-mile network that irrigated some 3,500 acres of land.

The best preserved of the acequias is located near Mission Espada. Espada Dam, which was completed in 1740 and is still in existence, diverted water from the river into a large trench (*acequia madre*, or mother ditch). To carry the water across nearby Piedras Creek, the Indians and missionaries built an arched stone aqueduct, Espada Aqueduct, which visitors can still see near Mission Espada. It is one of the oldest arched Spanish aqueducts in the United States.

The arches of the Espada Aqueduct, now more than 200 years old   (Courtesy of the National Park Service)

A water master, known as the *aguador*, controlled the flow of water to each field by opening and closing floodgates. The aguador also diverted water to power the mill wheels and for use in bathing and washing. Augmented by the addition of a modern dam, this 250-year-old system still provides water for use by nearby farms.

PRESERVING IT FOR THE FUTURE

Recognizing the cultural importance of the missions of San Antonio, the city began a concerted effort to preserve them in the 1920s. Through cooperative efforts of the Archdiocese of San Antonio, the San Antonio Conservation Society, the Texas Department of Parks and Wildlife, and several municipal agencies, these remnants of our national heritage have been maintained. The San Antonio Missions National Historic Park, more than 850 acres in size, was established in 1978, and since then the National Park Service has worked to stabilize the condition of the structures and preserve them.

The missions are open to the public, but a formal agreement between the National Park Service and the Archdiocese of San Antonio ensures that the traditional services at the four active parishes can continue undisturbed while visitors enjoy these sites.

EXPLORING ♦ FURTHER

Books about the San Antonio Missions and Spanish Missions in America

Hall, Douglas Kent. *Frontier Spirit: Early Churches of the Southwest.* New York: Abbeville Press, 1990.

Kalman, Bobbie. *Spanish Missions.* (Historic Communities) New York: Crabtree Publications, 1996.

Torres, Luis. *San Antonio Missions National Historical Park.* Tucson, Ariz.: Southwest Parks and Monuments, 1992.

Van Steenwyk, Elizabeth. *The California Missions.* (First Books) New York: Franklin Watts, 1995.

Wakely, David (photographer), and Thomas A. Drain. *A Sense of Mission: Historic Churches of the Southwest.* San Francisco: Chronicle Books, 1994.

Related Places

Carmel Mission Basilica
3080 Rio Road
Carmel, CA 93923

Established in 1770 by Father Junípero Serra, the Carmel Mission's original name is the Mission San Carlos Borromeo de Carmelo. It is the second in the chain of 21 California Missions. The most important of the California Spanish missions, it brought in some 4,000 Indians for baptism between 1770 and 1836. Located in the town of Carmel on the California coast, the mission was named for Saint Charles Borromeo, a leading Catholic reformer and humanitarian of the 16th century. The present stone structure was built on this site in 1793; by the following year, the mission enjoyed bountiful crops, and 794 Native Americans lived in the surrounding village. But the California missions never completed their planned cycle, due to many factors, both political and personal, and by 1834, the Carmel Mission's Indian population had dwindled to 381. The mission is now open to the public and remains as a monument to the Native Americans and Franciscan fathers who lived there, and to the heritage they contributed to American culture today.

The Alamo
P.O. Box 2599
San Antonio, TX 78299-2599
(210) 225-1391
Fax: (210) 229-1343

Of all the missions founded in San Antonio, Mission San Antonio de Valero was the first, established in 1718, and its purpose, like those that followed, was to spread Christianity among Native Americans who lived in the surrounding territory. The building that still stands in the heart of San Antonio was begun about 1755. But few people today know this place by its original name. The least successful of the original five missions, it was abandoned in 1793 and later renamed The Alamo (Spanish for "poplar" or "cottonwood"), after the home town of a garrison that occupied the mission in 1801. And it is by this name that Texas and the nation remembers it, because of the events that occurred there in April 1836—118 years after the mission's founding.

The Alamo became the scene of a bloody standoff between the Mexican dictator Antonio López de Santa Anna and a band of 189 rebellious Texans who stood their ground within the Alamo, demanding indepedence from Mexico. Faced with the approach of Santa Anna's army, which ultimately numbered 4,000, Colonel William Barret Travis unsheathed his sword and drew a line on the ground before his battle-weary men. Knowing the gravity of the moment he said, "Those prepared to give their lives in freedom's cause, come over to me." Every man except one crossed the line. Colonel James Bowie, ill with pneumonia, asked that his cot be carried over. From nearby Gonzalez, 32 men and boys had volunteered to join the Alamo's defenders, and many famous fighters were there that day, including David Crockett and his "Tennessee Boys." The following day, Santa Anna's army attacked from all directions at once. All 189 defenders died that day.

"Remember the Alamo!" became the Texans' rallying cry, and 46 days later 800 men under the leadership of General Sam Houston defeated Santa Anna's army of 1,500 at San Jacinto. Texas was free of Mexican rule, and a new republic was born. Texas remained an independent republic for 10 years, until it was officially annexed by the United States on December 29, 1845.

Grand Portage National Monument

VOYAGEUR RENDEZVOUS
Grand Portage, Minnesota

AT A GLANCE

Built: 1768

Fur trade site of the late 1700s

Reconstructed great hall, kitchen, and canoe warehouse, as well as a palisade wall of the rendezvous site and the 8½-mile Grand Portage, a gateway into the interior of North America that links Lake Superior with a secondary system of lakes and rivers.

Address:

Grand Portage National Monument
P.O. Box 668
315 South Broadway
Grand Marais, MN 55604
(218) 387-2788, voice or TDD
(218) 387-2790, fax

Just south of the Canadian border, this place known as Grand Portage [GRAHN PORTAHZH], or the "Great Carrying Place," served as rendezvous point for trappers and traders on their way around nearby High Falls and the other falls and rapids on the Pigeon River, as they headed upriver to the site of Fort Charlotte.

Beneath an hill . . . is the fort, picketed in with cedar pallisa-does, and inclosing houses built with wood and covered with shingles. They are calculated for every convenience of trade, as well as to accommodate the proprietors and clerks during their short residence there. . . .

—Alexander Mackenzie, explorer and trader, describing the North West Company's headquarters during a summer visit

♦ ♦ ♦ ♦ ♦

The Great Hall and Lookout Tower (Courtesy of the Grand Portage National Monument)

They called it "soft gold," and during the late 1700s it drew explorers, trappers, adventurers, entrepreneurs, and tradesmen in the hundreds to the northwestern shore of Lake Superior. Here, once a year at Grand Portage, the main headquarters of the North West Company, hard-headed business would mix with wild and raucous partying, while staid European businessmen cut deals and grizzled frontiersmen emerged from the deep woods to gather, trade, and shake off the loneliness of the long winter.

The "soft gold" was beaver, fox, and otter pelts, and during the height of the 1700s fur trade era, Grand Portage was, once each summer, the major meeting place for the traders, voyageurs, and trappers who made their living out of the vast North American interior.

The meeting place, or rendezvous at Grand Portage was a large 16-building stockade on the western shore of Lake Superior built in 1778 by the North West Company, a group of independent fur traders in competition with the British Hudson's Bay Company.

A crucial link on the water route from the profitable inland wilderness to Montreal, Canada, the capital city of the Great Lakes fur trade, Grand Portage, received its name from French explorers and missionaries sometime after 1722. Where streams were unnavigable, canoe men called voyageurs had to come ashore and carry their boats and cargo over a "portage," a trail that bypassed the unnavigable section. The Grand Portage provided safe passage around a dangerous section of the Pigeon River, the main thoroughfare from Lake Superior into the interior fur country. First developed by Native American travelers, this detour was an 8½-mile stretch of slippery muck, angry mosquitoes, and swarming black flies. The most strenuous of the 29 difficult portages that made up the entire water network, the Grand Portage was also an indispensable link in the chain that moved furs, goods, and trade back and forth between the interior and Montreal.

Quiet during the winter months, the North West Company's stockade at Grand Portage burst to life like a flowering plant every summer. The yearly cycle actually began in July, when brigades of voyageurs called "winterers" set out from Grand Portage carrying with them goods for their trading posts in the interior.

Through the harsh winter the men traded out of their isolated posts, exchanging European goods and other items for furs brought by the Indians. Then, as the ice on the rivers began to break up in mid-May they packed up

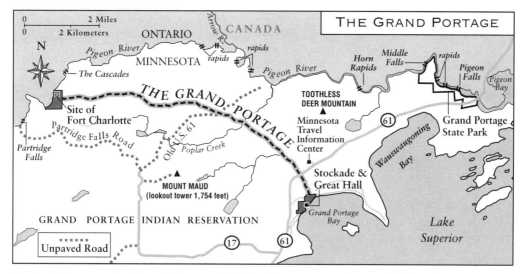

The trail known as the "Grand Portage" linked Lake Superior with Fort Charlotte, bypassing dangerous sections of the Pigeon River.

their valuable treasures of fur pelts and began the long and difficult journey back to the Grand Portage post. Meanwhile, another group of voyageurs, called the "Montrealers" or "pork-eaters," had set out from Montreal with more trade goods and were propelling their sturdy canoes up the Ottawa River and across the Great Lakes to the Grand Portage rendezvous site. Later, this group would make their way back to Montreal carrying the valuable cargoes of fur pelts, while the winterers would return to their trading posts with the goods that had been freshly ferried in. For both groups of voyageurs, the journey was long and dangerous.

Taking their name from the French word for traveler, the voyageurs of the fur trade era were a special breed of men. Though the majority were French, or French-Canadian, others were British, German, African, Russian, or Native American. What all had in common was a fierce pride in their work and a reputation for laboring energetically and without complaint no matter how difficult the circumstances. Both the pride and the reputation were well earned. The voyageurs' strength and endurance was legendary, eventually giving them the status of folk heroes. It was expected that a typical voyageur would work 14 hours a day, paddle 55 strokes a minute in a birch-bark canoe, and be able to carry two 90-pound bundles of furs across a rugged terrain of sharp rocks and slippery mud. They fell victims to disease, collapsed along

Carrying packs on the Grand Portage (Courtesy of the Grand Portage National Monument)

grueling portages, and drowned in the ice-cold waters of the wilderness. But in their minds they were free and proud men, living a life of purpose and adventure, far removed from the dull lives of clerks and city dwellers. And they would fight, at the drop of a hat, anyone who disputed the honor of their choice.

Given the hardships of the voyageurs' lives, it's little wonder then that the summer rendezvous at Grand Portage was a spectacular event. It's not hard to imagine today, wandering around the Grand Portage National Monument, what it must have been like during those summers in the late 1700s when as many as 800 to 1,000 voyageurs, fur-trading businessmen, company partners, clerks, and guides crowded into and around the Grand Portage stockade. Loud shouting, bartering, singing, arguing, and laughing filled the air inside and outside the stockade, and the entire area was a swirling kaleidoscopic mass of dust, dirt, and people in constant motion. Inside the Great Hall, business was being done by day, and the businessmen and clerks fed and entertained at night. Given the best treatment—after all they were the bosses, big-shots, and moneylenders—the fur-trading businessmen and company partners, wearing their city clothes, their expensive boots, and white shirts, sat down to dinner at the long tables and dined off fine Wedgwood china while they continued their deals and discussions. At other tables nearby the higher positioned company clerks talked politics and inventory and ate off of pewter plates while the newer and less important clerks, perhaps thinking of some home far away, made do with wooden cups and bowls. Singers, dancers, and musicians might entertain, and the best brandy and other alcoholic beverages were served with gracious abandon.

Alcohol was also present outside the Great Hall, probably in much greater abundance and certainly of much rougher quality. Great casks and chipped cups passed continuously from hand to hand and mouth to mouth. Sometimes the voyageurs would still be working, moving their bosses' great bundles of pelts from spot to spot, or repairing damaged canoes. But as often as not, while the business was being done in the Great Hall, the voyageurs would be using the time to relax and celebrate, greet old friends, and swap tall tales of their adventures during the long winter or along the dangerous portages. The sprawling flat area outside the stockade was perfect for quickly improvised games, dancing, and songfests. Drinking contests would be entered into at the slightest challenge, and fistfights were as common a source for wager as the rough-and-tumble games of tug-of-war. Late at night, as the last campfires in the encampment slowly burned down and the bosses and clerks slept inside the buildings of the stockade, the voyageurs would bed down in battered tents or under their birch-bark canoes and listen as lonely

Inside the Great Hall   (Courtesy of the Grand Portage National Monument)

singers strumming makeshift instruments sang nostalgic songs of lost loves and faraway lands.

The work was done energetically and honestly, the rendezvous was profitable for body and spirits, and the time off was lived to the fullest. It was a good time. And somehow it created a sense of pride—and that, for the voyageurs, made everything else seem worthwhile.

The Grand Portage stockade was abandoned in 1803, when the North West Company moved its trading center farther north in order to avoid taxation by the U.S. government. During its peak year in 1792, some 200,000 beaver skins passed through the stockade en route to Montreal, earning the owners around $70,000 in profit in an era when 5¢ was the cost of a pound of beef.

Although most of the 16 buildings that once occupied the site are now gone, the all-important Great Hall has been reconstructed, as have the

The Grand Portage Trail stretches 8½ miles over hilly terrain from Lake Superior to Fort Charlotte. (Courtesy of the Grand Portage National Monument)

kitchen, warehouse, dock, and palisade wall. Nearby, too, is the famous 8½-mile Grand Portage itself, which (except for an occasional board set down by a park ranger to provide safety over a rough spot) remains the same as it did over 200 years ago. In the warehouse outside the stockade you can see two of the same kind of birch-bark canoes used by the voyageurs, and an authentic reconstruction of a fur press, which was used to pack the bulky furs into easily handled bundles. Here, about 60 beaver pelts at a time were piled atop four binding cords and then, sandwiched in burlap or muslin, pressed and tied into the compact 90-pound bales carried by the voyageurs. Costumed interpreters offer demonstrations of canoe making, fur pressing, black-powder musket firing, and the songs and dances of the voyageurs. The truly hearty and adventurous can attempt to hike the long portage. Some make it, but even with today's lightweight and sturdy hiking shoes and without the disadvantage of two 90-pound bundles, most turn back to the stockade after only a few miles. Turning back wasn't an option the voyageurs had, though, and sometimes, just a few feet up the trail and around a bend, you might imagine you hear the sound of long-ago voices, continuing onward.

A CLOSE UP — THE BIRCH-BARK CANOES

Long before Europeans arrived, Indians used canoes for fishing, transporting trade goods, traveling to hunting grounds, and harvesting wild rice. From the materials they found around them—especially the bark of the birch and white cedar trees —they devised an ingenious transportation vehicle, the lightweight canoe.

Thanks to the resins it contains, birch bark is waterproof and extremely resistant to decay. White cedar, extremely light and strong, is the perfect wood for the ribs and framework of a canoe. The watercraft built by the Indians with these materials were perfect for navigation in the turbulent rivers of this region. They were also well suited for the portages around extremely rough waters, being relatively easy to carry.

When the French voyageurs arrived and first encountered the Lachine Rapids on the St. Lawrence River, they were quick to abandon their heavy three-masted sailing ships for the lightweight Indian canoes. The voyageurs adapted the 25-foot canoe, lengthening it to 36 feet, and expanded its carrying capacity. By using cargo poles in the bottom of the canoes, they were able to distribute the cargo weight evenly to prevent their craft from capsizing. These canoes were sleek, swift, and able to carry huge loads. Although the skin of the canoe was easily punctured, it could also be easily patched, and the canoe had the added advantage of serving as a shelter at night, when placed upside down over the voyageur's bedroll.

PRESERVING IT FOR THE FUTURE

Nearly 20 years after the Grand Portage post was abandoned, explorer David Thompson found only the remains of the foundations at what had once been a village teeming with activity. The Grand Portage trail was covered over by vegetation and fallen trees. The site remained in that condition until 1958, when the Grand Portage Band of Minnesota Ojibwa donated the land to the federal government, which declared the site a national monument that same year. Guided by written accounts and archaeological excavations, the National Park Service succeeded in reconstructing the exteriors of the buildings, furnishing the interiors in the style of 1797.

But the job was not over. On July 15, 1969, an enormous lightning strike ignited the reconstructed Great Hall, resulting in an uncontrollable inferno. In minutes, all the work was destroyed. However, reconstruction recommenced in 1971, based on new archaeological excavations, and the building reopened the following year. A newly discovered kitchen area was reconstructed and opened in 1975.

EXPLORING ◆ FURTHER

Books about Grand Portage and the Fur Trade

Amb, Thomas M. *The Voyageurs: Frontiersmen of the Northwest.* Minneapolis: T.S. Denision & Co., 1973.

Gilman, Carolyn. *The Grand Portage Story.* St. Paul: Minnesota Historical Society, 1992.

Hafen, LeRoy R. *Fur Traders, Trappers, and Mountain Men of the Upper Missouri.* Lincoln: University of Nebraska Press, 1995.

Larpenteur, Charles. *Forty Years a Fur Trader on the Upper Missouri: The Personal Narrative of Charles Larpenteur, 1833–1872*. Lincoln: University of Nebraska Press, 1989.

Related Places

Voyageurs National Park
3131 Highway 53
International Falls, MN 56649–8904
(218) 283-9821, headquarters
(218) 285-7407, fax

Voyageurs National Park was named for the French-Canadian canoemen who traveled these waters in their birch-bark canoes. The days of the voyageurs are long gone, but the waters they traveled remain and continue to influence and be influenced by people. From these waters and the accompanying scenery, geology, and rich cultural and natural resources Voyageurs National Park derives its national significance, preserved for the enjoyment of present and future generations.

Apostle Islands National Lakeshore
Route 1, Box 4
Bayfield, WI 54814
(715) 779-3397

This park includes 21 islands and 12 miles of mainland shoreline along Lake Superior, and the following sites are just two of several that are of historical interest, including the largest collection of lighthouses anywhere in the National Park System.

The Hokenson Fishery
Apostle Islands National Lakeshore
Route 1, Box 4
Bayfield, WI 54814
(715) 779-3397

The Hokenson Brothers Fishery stands on the shore of Lake Superior at Little Sand Bay. Operated for more than 30 years by the families of Eskel, Leo, and

Roy Hokenson, it was an enterprise that started from scratch and eventually prospered due to the Hokensons' resourcefulness, ingenuity, and hard work.

The Hokensons' story reads like a history of the Apostle Islands region. The three brothers were sons of Swedish immigrants. They grew up in Bayfield, where their father was involved in lumbering and brownstone quarrying. As young men Eskel, Leo, and Roy farmed and raised cattle on a family homestead near Little Sand Bay. Fishing originally provided an occasional change in diet, but after several unsuccessful years on the farm, the brothers began fishing commercially. By the late 1920s the Hokensons were farming during the day and fishing at night. Eventually they became more skillful at fishing and began to see a tidy profit. Soon they were fishing full-time. The Hokensons retired in the mid-1960s, and family members remaining in the area continue to be valuable sources of information about the fishery. Today, the fishery complex is maintained by the National Park Service. Its rustic buildings and historic artifacts are preserved as a museum where visitors can explore this remnant of the past.

Sand Island Light Station
Apostle Islands National Lakeshore
Route 1, Box 4
Bayfield, WI 54814
(715) 779-3397

One of several lighthouses within the Apostle Islands National Lakeshore along the edge of Lake Superior in Michigan, the Sand Island lighthouse began warning ships along the shore in 1892. Sand Island is the only lighthouse in the Apostles constructed of locally quarried brownstone. The light tower begins as a square rising from the northwest corner of the dwelling, then gracefully flows into an octagon surmounted by the lantern and walkway. Carved wood trim decorates the steeply sloped gable end of the quarters. This lighthouse, built in 1881, is an example of Norman Gothic, an architectural style associated with churches and town houses of the period.

Fort Clatsop

AT A GLANCE

Built: 1805

A stockade fort built by the Lewis and Clark expedition at the westernmost point in their famous expedition

This site celebrates the 1805–06 winter encampment of the 33-member Lewis and Clark expedition. The 125-acre park includes a replica of the 50-by-50-foot fort, reconstructed where it once stood, as well as the historic canoe landing and spring. Nearby, the Salt Works unit commemorates the expedition's salt-making activities in preparation for the journey back to the United States in 1806.

Address:
Fort Clatsop National Memorial
Route 3, Box 604-FC
Astoria, OR 97103
(503) 861-2471

Shortly after Thomas Jefferson's purchase of the vast Louisiana Territory from the French in 1803, Meriwether Lewis and William Clark set out with a party of guides to explore and map the great wilderness that had just become U.S. territory. Led across the Rocky Mountains by their Shoshone guide, Sacajawea, they descended the Salmon, Snake, and Columbia Rivers to the Pacific Ocean. There, in 1805, they constructed Fort Clatsop to shelter them until spring, when they would begin their return journey homeward.

At this place we . . . wintered and remained from the 7th Decr, 1805 to this day and have lived as well as we had a right to expect. . . .

—William Clark,
March 23, 1806

♦ ♦ ♦ ♦ ♦

Daily activities for the explorers during their winter at Fort Clatsop included woodworking, laundering, and standing watch. (Courtesy of the National Park Service, photo by Curt Johnson)

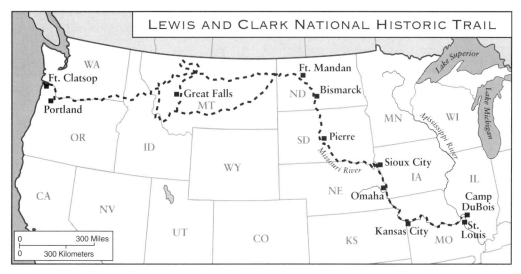

Map of Lewis and Clark Trail and location of Fort Clatsop. The members of Lewis and Clark's "Corps of Discovery" built Fort Clatsop at the far western end of their route of exploration through the newly acquired U.S. Louisiana Territory and lands beyond.

W hen Meriwether Lewis and William Clark set up their rough winter camp near the mouth of the Columbia River in what is now northwestern Oregon, they had reached the western turnaround of a long journey that had begun by flatboat and keelboat up the Missouri River in the spring of 1804. With a contingent of 45 volunteers, the expedition had traveled some 1,100 miles up the Missouri to winter near the site of present-day Bismarck, North Dakota. There they were joined by Sacajawea, a Shoshone woman who volunteered as interpreter, and her husband, Toussaint Charbonneau. The expedition had then followed the Missouri westward to its headwaters and crossed the Rocky Mountains to proceed along the Salmon, Snake, and Columbia Rivers to a site the explorers called Fort Clatsop in honor of the nearby Clatsop Indian tribe. The plan was to winter there, within sight of the Pacific Ocean, and then begin their long journey back home. They would use the time to work on their journals, draw detailed maps, and prepare scientific accounts of what they had accomplished thus far on their expedition, one of the most successful and fruitful explorations in the history of the United States.

The fledgling United States had nearly doubled in size in 1803 when President Thomas Jefferson bought from France most of the land between

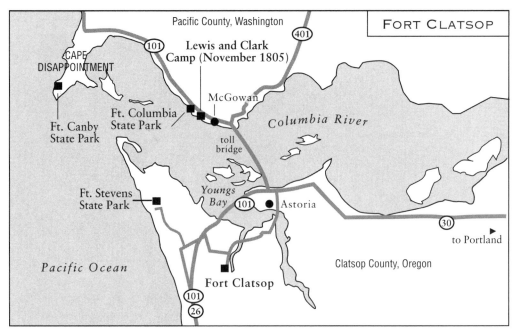

Located near the mouth of the Columbia River, Fort Clatsop was within a short distance of the mighty Pacific Ocean.

the Mississippi River and the Rocky Mountains. Since winning its independence from England the United States had sought free access down the Mississippi to the Gulf of Mexico. Negotiations had been under way with the Spanish, who had owned the territory since 1795, but in 1801, President Jefferson learned that Spain had secretly ceded the Louisiana Territory to France.

The French emperor Napoléon had hoped to build a new French empire in North America, but his plans had gone awry after a slave revolt in French Haiti and an impending French War with England left France badly in need of money. For $15 million, or approximately 4¢ an acre, the United States acquired about 828,000 square miles. The boundaries of the purchase were roughly set, with the Mississippi River forming the eastern limit and the gulf of Mexico the southern; further treaties defined the northern boundary as reaching to Canada and the western border extending to the middle of present-day Montana.

The acquisition was a coup, although some thought it a rash move, and the president was eager to investigate and prove the value of his purchase.

Jefferson authorized an expedition in 1804 to explore the newly acquired territory and report back on its value.

Jefferson chose Meriwether Lewis to head the expedition. Lewis, who had earned a captain's rank in the military, had also served as Jefferson's private secretary in 1801 and had read Jefferson's State of the Union message to Congress in December of that year. He was keenly intelligent, something of a dreamer, and a little aloof. He had also spent his childhood in the rural areas of Vermont, and during his military career he had acquired valuable knowledge of Native American character and customs. Under the informal tutelage of Jefferson, he had also refined his already keen interest in plants and animals.

Viewing the Pacific Ocean from Tillamook Head, much as the Lewis and Clark expedition did in 1805–06. (Courtesy of the National Park Service, photo by Curt Johnson)

Jefferson had made a wise choice. And so did Lewis when he selected his close friend William Clark, the younger brother of the Revolutionary War hero George Rogers Clark, to share with him the leadership role of the expedition. Also a military man before resigning from the army to travel and tend his estate, William Clark had fought in many Indian campaigns and was well acquainted with the rough-and-tumble life. His outgoing personality also complemented that of the sometimes moody and introspective Lewis.

When at last the expedition arrived at the western edge of the continent, both Lewis and Clark—and all the rest of the party—were buoyant over the immense achievement. On that day—November 7, 1805—this entry appeared in the journals of Lewis and Clark: "Great Joy . . . we are in view of

Everything needed for daily life had to be found, hunted, or made by hand. Here, a ranger pulls tallow for candles in the same way Lewis and Clark's party made candles for light during the winter of 1805–06. (Courtesy of the National Park Service, photo by Curt Johnson)

Interior of the captain's quarters   (Courtesy of the National Park Service, photo by Curt Johnson)

the ocean . . . which we (have) been so long anxious to see, and the roaring or noise made by the waves breaking on the rocky shores . . . may be heard distinctly."

The first camp, set up by the expedition in November 1805 on the Washington side of the Columbia River, hadn't turned out to be a poor choice. But within 10 days Lewis and Clark had decided to abandon this preliminary camp on the north shore and cross to the other side, moving a little farther south, where they believed that elk and other food supplies would be more plentiful. Lewis took a small party and crossed over to explore the area until he found a more suitable site for their winter quarters. There was game there, enough for a long winter, and a badly needed supply of salt. On December 8 the explorers began to build their fort, approximately 3 miles up the Netul (now the Lewis and Clark) River.

Today, when visitors explore the campsite on foot, it requires only a small stretch of the imagination to follow in the footsteps of the expedition members as they went about their daily tasks. On a mild, balmy day, though, it may be more difficult to envision the hard, wet winter weather that plagued them. Of the 106 days that the Lewis and Clark expedition spent at Fort Clatsop, only 12 were free of rain. Even inside the walls of the fort, clothing rotted and dampness permeated every hour of every day. There are no fleas, now, but at that time they infested everything so severely that both Lewis and Clark wrote often of their inability to get a full night's sleep.

The present fort, nestled in the lush forest, is a replica based on the original roughly drawn floor plan etched by William Clark in the cover of his field book. It immediately calls to mind the expedition's strong military origin. Within a log stockade 50 feet square, two rows of cabins (three rooms on the west side and four on the east) are separated by a parade ground. The original had been constructed mostly of felled timber, supplemented by sections commandeered from an abandoned Indian structure found nearby. Visiting Fort Clatsop today, you can amble through its once crowded and hectic rooms. You can explore the quarters set aside for the volunteer enlisted men; the captain's quarters, which served as office and sleeping area for Lewis and Clark; and the storeroom where meat, trading items, and other supplies were kept. You'll find the orderly room much as it was when it served as headquarters for the guard detail. And you can look into what is now called the Charbonneau Room, which housed Toussaint Charbonneau and his wife, Sacajawea, and their infant son, Jean-Baptiste. You can climb into the sentry box, which was built as protection for the soldier on guard duty.

During the cold, wet winter most of the activity inside Clatsop centered around the captain's quarters, where Lewis and Clark worked on their journals and maps documenting the journey. The rest of their time was spent tending the fort's day-by-day management—not an easy job. Illness from the cold and injuries were a regular problem, and hunting expeditions had to be sent out constantly to replenish the food supplies, which rotted quickly. Their journals reveal that the expedition members killed and ate 131 elk, 20 deer, and a number of smaller animals during the winter, but keeping the meat fresh was a major problem. The damp weather was cold enough to make everyone uncomfortable, but not cold enough to adequately preserve their food.

The trappers accompanying Lewis and Clark used long rifles like the one these men are working on. (Courtesy of the National Park Service, photo by Curt Johnson)

Food was also replenished in trade with the local Indians who made regular visits to the camp, and Lewis and Clark used these occasions to study each tribe, recording in their journals valuable information about the Indians' appearance, habits, living conditions, and lodging. They also wrote admiringly about the Indians' abilities as hunters and fishermen, and most of the trading items brought along by the expedition were quickly depleted in exchange for fresh food. At one point the Indians even brought in blubber from a beached whale and offered it for trade. Though Clark recorded that he didn't care much for the taste, he was quickly off the next morning to examine the whale and make what observations he could.

Another of the winter's major activities was the procurement of much-needed salt, which had run low on the expedition's journey westward. "We having fixed on this situation as the one best calculated for our winter quarters," Clark wrote in his journal, "I determined to go as direct a course as I could to the seacoast." Clark's main purpose was to find a route for a salt-making party. Although Clark himself was indifferent to salted food, the majority of the expedition wanted it as seasoning, and since their usual fare often left much to be desired, he was anxious to keep the expedition's morale up. You can visit the expedition's saltworks today by driving 15 miles southwest from Fort Clatsop to a spot on the seacoast near the small town of Seaside, a journey now much easier than it was in Lewis and Clark's time.

There, near some lodgings of the Clatsop and Tillamook people, they "commenced the makeing of salt and found that they could make from three quarts to a gallon a day," Clark wrote, calling it "excellent, white and fine."

Three men working constantly at the salt site, using five brass kettles to boil approximately 1,400 gallons of seawater, produced over three and a half bushels of salt in only a few weeks.

Having survived the harsh winter with no loss of life, and having done a great deal of work in further studies as well as compiling official records of their journey west, Lewis and Clark abandoned Fort Clatsop in the spring of 1806. Much more would be accomplished and learned on their long trek home.

Today, standing at Clatsop, the most westward point in Lewis and Clark's journey, visitors experience a quiet awe at the humble fort site as they reflect on the accomplishments of the historic expedition. Before Lewis and Clark's explorations, the Louisiana Territory had been a vast, uncharted area of "rumor, guess and fantasy." With the successful completion of their mission, the two leaders and all the brave adventurers of their party had given the people of the United States much more than a light in the wilderness. They had fashioned an entirely new approach to exploration by systematically recording precise data on such subjects as flora, fauna, geography, and the weather. They studied and recorded valuable information on Indian tribes and customs. Their topographical studies and maps became major sources for information and further exploration, and their reports on the abundance of beaver and other fur-bearing animals helped to open up the Northwest to American fur traders and settlers. Much more, though, lay ahead as a direct result of their endeavor, for thanks to the Lewis and Clark expedition the nation also came into contact with much of its future potential—the great corn fields of Iowa, Missouri, Kansas, and Nebraska, the vast wheat country of the Dakotas, the gold and silver mines of Montana, and the mighty forests of Washington and Oregon.

Perhaps, with all this in mind, standing outside Clatsop or stopping near the fresh spring where the expedition drew its water or the canoe landing where the explorers first stepped ashore, the visitor can sense the magnitude of this magnificent adventure, an expedition not only into America's wilderness but also into its future.

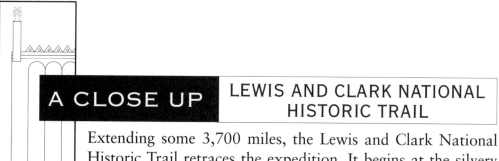

A CLOSE UP — LEWIS AND CLARK NATIONAL HISTORIC TRAIL

Extending some 3,700 miles, the Lewis and Clark National Historic Trail retraces the expedition. It begins at the silvery arch of the Jefferson National Expansion Memorial in St. Louis, Missouri, and extends through Missouri, Kansas, Iowa, Nebraska, South Dakota, North Dakota, Montana, Idaho, and Washington to its western terminus, Fort Clatsop at the mouth of the Columbia River in Oregon. Markers—maintained through cooperative efforts by local, county, state, and federal governments, as well as nonprofit organizations and private landowners—indicate the exact route, up rivers and waterways, across mountains, down what now are highways and byways across the American countryside. Travelers wanting to retrace the entire journey must be ready to change modes of transportation—perhaps hiking or riding bicycles or horseback across the Lolo Pass between Montana and Idaho, boating or rafting on rivers, and in some cases traveling by car.

Even following a portion of the trail gives you an idea of how exciting Lewis and Clark's first venture must have been. Many resources exist for those interested in knowing more about the trail or in traveling its impressive length. A good place to begin is with the general brochure offered by the National Park Service, available from Lewis and Clark National Historic

Trail, 700 Rayovac Drive, Suite 100, Madison, Wisconsin 53711 (or telephone 608-264-5610, 8A.M.–5P.M., Monday through Friday. E-mail to the Lewis and Clark National Historic Trail may be directed to **Richard_Williams@nps.gov.**)

The NPS can also help with information about planning, coordination, and NPS administration and programs. Additionally, a semiannual Lewis and Clark National Historic Trail administrative update is available upon request.

The Lewis and Clark Trail Heritage Foundation is a nonprofit organization with a national membership dedicated to the preservation of the heritage of the Lewis and Clark expedition. The organization publishes a quarterly magazine, *We Proceeded On,* and holds an annual meeting at a Lewis and Clark site. You can find out more about the preservation and interpretation of the trail from the Lewis and Clark Trail Heritage Foundation. Membership in the Foundation is open to the public, and volunteers are welcome. You can contact either the NPS or the Foundation directly.

For more information write: Lewis and Clark Trail Heritage Foundation, P.O. Box 3434, Great Falls, Montana 59403.

PRESERVING IT FOR THE FUTURE

In 1955 on the 150th anniversary of Lewis and Clark's arrival on the Pacific coast, local citizens constructed a replica of Fort Clatsop. Based on Captain Clark's original floor plan, it now nestles amid second-growth timber, the old forest having been cut down long ago. Even though archaeological digs have proved inconclusive, historians believe the reconstruction is faithful, based as it is on the recollections of settlers and the writings and maps done by Lewis and Clark at the time of their expedition.

In 1958 the National Park Service acquired the 125-acre site as a memorial to Lewis and Clark's "Corps of Discovery," as they called their team of enlisted soldiers, nonmilitary hunters, and interpreters. This remarkable group included Sacajawea, a Native American and the expedition's only female member, and York, Clark's African-American servant.

Books about Fort Clatsop and the Lewis and Clark Expedition

Clark, William, and Meriwether Lewis. *Off the Map: The Journals of Lewis and Clark*. Edited by Peter Roop. New York: Walker & Co. Library, 1993.

Dattilio, Daniel J. *Fort Clatsop: The Story Behind the Scenery*. Edited by Russell D. Butcher. Las Vegas, Nev.: KC Publications, 1986.

McGrath, Patrick. *The Lewis and Clark Expedition*. (Turning Points in American History) Morristown, N.J.: Silver Burdett Press, 1985.

Twist, Clint. *Lewis and Clark: Exploring the Northwest*. (Beyond the Horizons) Austin, Texas: Raintree/Steck Vaughn, 1994.

Related Place

Cabrillo National Monument
1800 Cabrillo Memorial Drive
San Diego, CA 92106-3601
Voice: (619) 557-5450; TDD: (619) 224-4140
Fax: (619) 557-5469

On September 28, 1542, Juan Rodríguez Cabrillo landed at San Diego Bay. This landing marked the first time Europeans set foot on what later became the west coast of the United States. He later steered his ship northward and explored along the uncharted coastline of California. It was the first step toward colonizing the expanded Spanish empire, which now extended to the Pacific Ocean. The Cabrillo National Monument was established in 1913 to commemorate Cabrillo's accomplishments as an explorer.

Fort Ross State Historic Park

RUSSIAN TRADING OUTPOST ON THE PACIFIC
Jenner, California

AT A GLANCE

Built: 1811

Site where Russian fur traders settled in 1811,
the southernmost outpost of Russian presence in America

Reconstructions of settlement buildings, including a stockade and fort,
as well as the fort's Russian Orthodox chapel, which was destroyed
in the earthquake of 1906

Address:
Fort Ross State Historic Park
19005 Coast Highway 1
Jenner, CA 95450
(707) 847-3286

> Before the Russians arrived in 1811, this location was the site of a Kashaya Pomo Indian village. According to one account, the entire area was acquired from the natives for "three blankets, three pairs of breeches, two axes, three hoes, and some beads." Considered suitable for settlement due to its plentiful water, good forage, and a nearby supply of wood for the necessary construction, this site was also relatively far from the Spanish, whose northernmost settlement was in the San Francisco Bay area. Because Spain, France, and Great Britain were occupied with major wars, no colonial power was ready to block the Russian move south into Spanish California. In fact, it was several months before the leaders of the Spanish settlement were even aware of the development at Fort Ross, and by then it was too late—the fort was completed, well armed, and vigilantly manned.

Can you imagine what it would have been like, as a Kashaya child from the interior, coming to Ross for the first time to visit relatives or trade? I picture the child walking through the villages, seeing strange houses and people, trying new foods, hearing foreign languages, listening to the music, the songs, the laughter. It would have been like a carnival, with everything bright and new, awaiting discovery. In those early years at Ross Settlement, communication would have been incredibly important, as people with many past differences became a single community working together. Their success and survival depending on communication, cultural sharing, and goodwill. I would have liked to have seen Ross Settlement in those early years, especially as a child.

—E. Breck Parkman, archaeologist, 1997

♦ ♦ ♦ ♦ ♦

Fort Ross sits on the rugged California coast, 70 miles north of San Francisco, and 11 miles northwest of the small town of Jenner. A wooden stockade with 14-foot-high weather-beaten redwood walls, its main gate faces west over the Pacific Ocean toward the coast of Russia, more than 5,000 miles away. Here on this windy and often fog-shrouded bluff, for over 30 years a permanent encampment of Russians, native Alaskans, people of mixed Russian and native Alaskan ancestry, and native Californians worked and made their homes. What were they doing here, the majority of them so far from home?

The story of Fort Ross started far to the north in 1763. That year Russian fur traders crossed the Bering Strait to settle on Kodiak Island in the Gulf of Alaska. Hunting and trading in this region proved immediately profitable, and by 1784 a Russian by the name of Gregory Shelekov had founded the first permanent Russian settlement in Alaska at Three Saints Bay. In 1799, Shelekov created the Russian-American Company and convinced the czar of Russia to give his firm a complete monopoly over all Russian fur trading in North America. To encourage this support, Shelekov gave the czar and his family large blocks of stock in the company. With the competition virtually

This Orthodox cross marks the site of the cemetery serving the Fort Ross settlement. It is echoed by the crosses of the reconstructed Orthodox chapel inside the fort's stockade. (Courtesy of the Fort Ross Interpretive Association, Inc., photo by Daniel F. Murley)

eliminated, Shelekov's company expanded quickly, and by 1804 the Russian-American Company moved its base of operations to Sitka, which the Russians called New Archangel.

Two other important figures entered the story at around this time: Alexander Baranov, an employee of the Russian-American Company since its founding and a resident of North America since 1799, and Nikolai Rezanov, an imperial inspector of the Russian-American Company who arrived in Sitka in 1805. Baranov had expanded the company's operations by engaging native Alaskan hunters to travel south on American ships to hunt sea otters along the coast of California—a single otter pelt, sold in Canton, China could bring enough to pay the salary of a Russian clerk for a full year.

Although the pelt hunting was good, the Russian colony was often short on food, and things were particularly bad at the time of Rezanov's arrival. So Rezanov convinced Baranov to allow him to sail down the coast toward Spanish California in search of supplies.

Here the story took first a romantic and then a tragic turn. After sailing his ship, the *Juno*, past the Spanish guns and into the harbor of San Francisco Bay, Rezanov attempted to convince the Spanish to trade with him. The Spanish, who had a standing policy of not permitting foreign ships to trade in California, steadfastly refused. Six weeks of negotiating resolved nothing. But romance did. When Rezanov proposed marriage to Concepción Arguello, the teenage daughter of the Spanish commander at San Francisco, the impasse was quickly broken, and within a few days the *Juno* was loaded with supplies.

Rezanov was a member of the Russian Orthodox Church, and the Spanish commander had to obtain permission from the Vatican before his daughter could marry a non-Catholic. So the happy couple's plans were put on temporary hold while Rezanov sailed northward back to Sitka with his shipload of supplies.

Rezanov brought more than fresh supplies and news of his upcoming wedding when he arrived back at Sitka. His journey into Spanish California had convinced him of the need to establish regular trade relations with the Spanish. But he also saw that the Russians needed a trading base of their own along the coast just north of the Spanish territory. Baranov, delighted at Rezanov's success, was quickly convinced and dispatched Ivan Kuskov, a

The reconstructed stockade and buildings of Fort Ross, Russian outpost on the California coast
(Courtesy of the Fort Ross Interpretive Association, Inc., photo by Daniel F. Murley)

long-time company employee, on another southward voyage to establish a possible location for the company's California settlement.

Meanwhile, Rezanov, still awaiting news from the Vatican, decided to cross the Bering Strait again and journey overland to St. Petersburg, Russia's imperial capital. He never made it. While crossing Siberia he was thrown from his horse and killed. According to traditional accounts, Rezanov's bride to be learned of his death only six years later. Then, heartbroken, she entered a Dominican convent, where she spent the remainder of her life.

Kuskov, meanwhile, had sailed into Bodega Bay, 70 miles north of the northernmost Spanish outpost at San Francisco. Arriving on January 8, 1804, with his company of 40 Russians and 150 Alaskan natives, he spent six months exploring the area and collecting over 2,000 valuable sea otter pelts.

It wasn't until 1811, however, that the Russians sailed southward again with plans to set up a permanent colony. With Kuskov again heading the expedition, they arrived at Bodega Bay, north of San Francisco, in March of 1812 aboard a ship called the *Chirikov*. After a little further exploration, Koskov decided that the best place to build the permanent Russian settlement was the site of a Kashaya Indian village 18 miles to the north. The local Indians called the spot Meteni, and according to one account it was quickly "acquired" from its owners for the sum of "three blankets, three pairs of breeches, two axes, three hoes, and some beads."

Whether the peaceful Kashaya were more impressed with Kuskov's trade goods or with his armed company of 25 Russians and 80 Alaskans is not known, but within days Kuskov had his men setting up a temporary camp on the site of the Indian village, while they began to build houses and a sturdy wooden blockade—the colony and fortification of Ross.

Kuskov was happy with his site; it offered a harbor of sorts, an abundant supply of water, and a good supply of nearby wood for construction. It was also strategically situated in relation to the Spanish at San Francisco—far enough away to permit a margin of safety, but near enough to try and organize trade. The stockade and one building were completed in a few months and formally dedicated on August 13, 1812. It is generally believed today that the name "Ross" was a shortened version of "Rossiya," the Russia of czarist days.

The Russian colony at Fort Ross lasted for nearly 30 years. During that time most of its activities centered around the hunting of sea otter pelts by the Kodiak islanders who eventually came, along with local Indians, to make up the colony's majority population. Only a small number of Russians actually lived at Ross, and there were never many Russian women other than the wives of a few officials. Intermarriage between Russians and natives of Alaska and California was commonplace; the local natives, people of mixed ancestry, and lower-ranking company men all lived in the village complex of 60 to 70 buildings just outside the stockade walls. The hunters and their families lived in their own village on a bluff overlooking the ocean just west of the main stockade.

Soon after its founding, Ross was an active and profitable colony. Although the Spanish had declared trading with the colony illegal, commerce between Spaniards and Russians took place all the same, with mutual benefit. For a number of years the marine hunting was good, as the Kodiak Islanders and their Russian overseers ranged the coast from Baja California to Oregon.

Just as quickly, though, it all came to an end. By the 1820s the slaughter of sea otters had almost completely depleted the otter population, and the colony was forced to rely on agriculture and stock raising as its primary occupations. The Russian-American Company's outposts in the north still needed to be supplied, but once the sea otter population had vanished, Ross was poorly suited to meet those needs. Most of the Alaskans, who depended on otter pelts for income, returned north. The thick ocean fogs made heavy agriculture difficult, and ravenous gophers and mice overran the fields. The Russians were also unable to drum up any real interest in farming among the proud native Californians, who had no interest in farming. Some attempts were made to set up small ranches and sites further inland, but without the sea otters the Ross colonists still couldn't produce enough to make a profit.

The Rotchev house survives as the only remaining structure at Fort Ross that was built during the Russian period (1812–41). (Courtesy of the Fort Ross Interpretive Association, Inc., photo by Daniel F. Murley)

The death blow for the colony came in 1839, when the Russian-American Company signed an agreement with the Hudson's Bay Company to supply Sitka with provisions from its settlements in present day Washington and Oregon. With no reason left for its existence, the Ross colony was disbanded. After trying with little success to sell the property to the Mexican government, the Russian-American Company made a deal with John Sutter, a naturalized Mexican citizen who had established a settlement called New Helvetia in what is now Sacramento, California. Sutter agreed to pay the Russian-American Company the equivalent of $30,000 in shipments of wheat over a three-year period. In return, Sutter sent his assistants to Fort Ross, where they quickly gathered up arms, ammunition, hardware, and other valuables, including over 2,000 head of cattle, as well as sheep and other animals, and transported them to Sutter's Fort in Sacramento.

Today, what remains of Fort Ross is pretty much what was left after Sutter stripped the property. A succession of owners, age, and natural disasters have taken their toll, but you can still feel the Russian and Alaskan Native presence as you wander inside the stockade walls. Two octagonal blockhouses with portholes for cannons stand at the southeast and northwest corners of the fort, and two jet-black artillery pieces point seaward. On the walls inside a building once used by visiting officials, seal and otter pelts hang above wooden casks marked in Cyrillic characters.

Kuskov House, the home of the company's first manager and most of his successors, stands between the northwestern blockhouse and the chapel, built in the 1820s. The Rotchev House stands near the West Gate. It is the only original Russian structure at Fort Ross, believed to be the oldest European-built wooden structure west of the Mississippi. Built in the 1830s for the last manager, Alexander Gavrilovich Rotchev, and his wife, the former princess Elena Gagarina, the house at one time boasted, according to a visitor, "a choice library, a piano, and a score of Mozart."

Today the only music heard is that of the nearby pounding sea—just outside the stockade walls to the right of the East Gate, you can see Sandy Beach Cove. Here the Russians loaded and unloaded their boats, a type of open, skin-covered boat they called a *baidara*, which they rowed to and from Bodega Bay, about 18 miles to the south, where large incoming and outgoing ships were able to anchor. In this area there were also a number of buildings, including a tannery, boat shop, and boathouse where the Russians built three brigs, a schooner, and some smaller boats, the first ships ever built in California. It is unknown whether any of these ships were used to remove the last of the Russians when they abandoned the settlement. But nearby, across a small gulch, over 100 Russian Orthodox crosses mark the site of the settlement's cemetery, and wandering here, just outside the old fort, among the graves of those who never returned home, you can turn once more toward the sea and appreciate just how far away home must have seemed.

A CLOSE UP — A RUSSIAN ORTHODOX CHAPEL ON THE PACIFIC

One of the most distinctive features of Fort Ross is the Russian Orthodox chapel, built of native redwood. What we see today is a reconstruction—authentically executed, although not the original. Because Fort Ross is located close to the San Andreas Fault, it suffered greatly during the great 1906 earthquake that demolished San Francisco. All of the fort's remaining buildings suffered some damage, but most seriously hit was the chapel. The foundation crumbled and the walls were ruined, and only the roof and two towers remained intact.

Between 1916 and 1918, the chapel was rebuilt, using timbers from both the officials' quarters and the warehouse. However, in 1970 a fire destroyed the chapel once again. Supporters of Fort Ross sponsored a new restoration, which was completed in 1974. Following Russian Orthodox tradition, some lumber from the burned building was used. The original bell, which was located to the left of the chapel, had melted in the fire, but restorers had it recast in Belgium using some of the original metals. In 1925 the chapel began to be used for Orthodox religious services, and it continues to be used for services every Memorial Day and Fourth of July.

Old Russian well (foreground) and the chapel. This Russian Orthodox chapel is a reconstruction of the one built in the 1820s during the time when Fort Ross was settled by the Russian-American Company. It was the first Russian Orthodox chapel built south of Alaska in North America. (Courtesy of the Fort Ross Interpretive Association, Inc., photo by Daniel F. Murley)

PRESERVING IT FOR THE FUTURE

In 1873 the area where Fort Ross once stood became part of the 15,000-acre Call Ranch, established by George W. Call. A wharf was built from the foot of the bluff to the cove and a 180-foot chute carried lumber and bulk cargo to ships anchored in the bay. In addition to logging, the ranch produced dairy products, vegetables, and fruit.

The Call family held the property until 1903, when the California Historical Landmarks Committee purchased the fort and three acres of surrounding land. The site was turned over to the State of California for

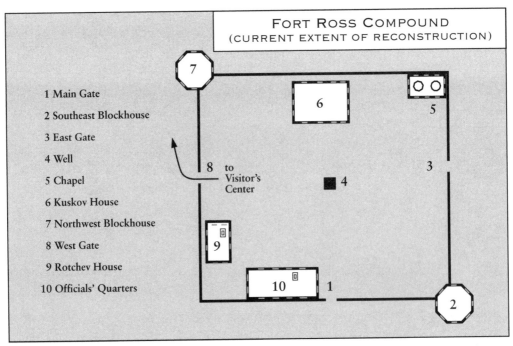

1 Main Gate

2 Southeast Blockhouse

3 East Gate

4 Well

5 Chapel

6 Kuskov House

7 Northwest Blockhouse

8 West Gate

9 Rotchev House

10 Officials' Quarters

Plans call for continued reconstruction and archaeological excavation of this lovely 19th-century Russian outpost on the California coast.

preservation and restoration as a state historic monument in March 1906. A short time later, the great earthquake of 1906 extensively damaged the chapel, the barracks, and the stockade wall. Since then, the California Department of Parks and Recreation has carried out restoration and reconstruction work, so that today you can see Fort Ross as it looked when the Russians lived and worked here. Plans call for the eventual reconstruction of more buildings.

EXPLORING ♦ FURTHER

Books and Articles about Fort Ross, the Russian Presence, and the Kashaya People

Kalani, Lyn, Lynn Rudy, and John Sperry, editors. *Fort Ross.* Fort Ross, Calif.: Fort Ross Interpretive Association, 1997.

Lightfoot, Kent G., Thomas A. Wake, and Ann M. Schiff. "Native Responses to the Russian Mercantile Colony of Fort Ross, Northern California," *Journal of Field Archaeology*, 20: 1993, pp. 159–175.

———. *The Archaeology and Ethnohistory of Fort Ross, California.* Berkeley: Archaeological Research Facility, University of California at Berkeley, 1991 (vol. 1) and 1997 (vol. 2).

Magocsi, Paul R. *The Russian Americans.* New York: Chelsea House Publishers, 1989.

Sweetland Smith, Barbara, and Redmond J. Barnett, editors. *Russian America: The Forgotten Frontier.* Olympia: Washington State Historical Society, 1990.

Thompson, Robert A. *The Russian Settlement in California, Fort Ross; Founded 1812, Abandoned 1841: Why the Russians Came and Why They Left.* Oakland, Calif.: Biobooks, 1951.

Watrous, Stephen. *Outpost of an Empire, Fort Ross: The Russian Colony in California.* Fort Ross, Calif.: Fort Ross Interpretive Association, 1993.

Related Places

Sitka National Historical Park
106 Metlakatla Street
Box 738
Sitka, AK 99835
(907) 747-6281
Fax: (907) 747-5938

This historic park, Alaska's oldest federally designated park, was established in 1910 to commemorate the Battle of Sitka, which took place in 1804 between Russian fur traders and the natives of Alaska's northwest coast. All that remains of this last major conflict is the site of Kiksadi Fort, located within the confines of this scenic 107-acre park in a temperate rain forest. The historic saga continues in a second unit of the park, at the Russian Bishop's House in Sitka, one of four surviving examples of Russian colonial architecture in North America. This original 1843 log structure conveys the legacy of Russian America through exhibits, refurbished living quarters, and the Chapel of the Annunciation.

Sutter's Fort
2701 L St.
Sacramento, CA 95816
(916) 445-4422 or 324-0539

John Sutter bought the property of Fort Ross, but not the land itself. He then removed more than 2,000 head of livestock, small buildings, threshing floors, muskets, and other equipment to Sutter's Fort at the junction of the American and Sacramento Rivers. Sutter's Fort is now a state museum, open to the public.

Fort Larned

PROTECTING THE SANTA FE TRAIL
Larned, Kansas

AT A GLANCE

Built: 1859

Fort built to defend the Santa Fe Trail

Located in southwestern Kansas, six miles west of the city of Larned, this fort was established to protect settlers and merchandise traveling along the Santa Fe Trail, which led westward through the Southwest to California. Nine buildings remain, including a reconstructed blockhouse.

Address:
Fort Larned National Historic Site and Museum
Route 3
Larned, KS 67550
(316) 285-6911

Two miles from Fort Larned, visitors can still see the ruts of the Santa Fe Trail, worn deep by the wagon wheels of westward-traveling pioneers and merchants. By 1859 the army had established a fort (moved the following year to the present location) to provide escort for those traveling the dangerous route through unfriendly lands.

The overland trade between the United States and the northern province of Mexico, seems to have had no very definite origin; having been rather the result of accident than of any organized plan of commercial establishment.

—Josiah Gregg (1806–50), trader, army agent,
and translator in the Southwest

◆ ◆ ◆ ◆ ◆

Fort Larned, protector of the Santa Fe Trail, was a small collection of modest buildings arranged symmetrically in the midst of the vast flatlands of Kansas—completely unprotected by fence or barricade. (photo by American Images, Marshfield, Wisconsin)

As Americans moved westward in search of new opportunities in the 19th century, they took many routes. The Santa Fe Trail, stretching 780 miles from Independence, Missouri, to Santa Fe, New Mexico, quickly became one of the most heavily traveled. Along these rutted traces moved stage lines and merchandise, as well as miners, cowboys, buffalo hunters, farmers, and merchants.

Originally opened up by William Becknell in 1821, the trail actually comprised two main routes with a number of variations. Both routes ran westward across Kansas to the Arkansas River, then followed the river southwest to a crossing west of Dodge City. From there, one fork of the trail, called the Mountain Fork, continued along the Arkansas River to a point near La Junta, Colorado, and then turned south through the mountains and Raton Pass to Fort Union. The other main route, called the Cimarron Fork, crossed the river just west of Dodge City and then continued southwest through the waterless plains country and into Fort Union. From Fort Union both routes turned south around the Sangre de Cristo Mountains, and then moved northwest into Santa Fe.

From 1822 to 1880, the Santa Fe Trail remained one of the most important overland routes to the West. New southwestern territories opened up after the Mexican War (1846–48) and the gold rushes of 1849 and 1858, adding to the already steady westward migration. Since the trail crossed over lands occupied by Native Americans, there was bound to be trouble. Seeing their lands and ways of life threatened by the influx of white travelers, the tribes fought back by attacking wagon trains, mail shipments, and commercial traffic.

To protect the trade route and its travelers, the United States government established a number of military posts along the trail, among them Fort Larned in southwestern Kansas. Today, with its nine original stone buildings, this fort is both a colorful survivor of the famous Indian Wars period and a sobering link with our nation's often violent and controversial past.

In its time Larned hosted such legendary western figures as Kit Carson, "Buffalo Bill" Cody, George Armstrong Custer, and the heroic African-American troopers of the 10th Cavalry, known as the Buffalo Soldiers.

For several critical years of America's westward expansion the fort was the principle guardian of the Santa Fe Trail, as its soldiers, working with troops from Fort Union and Fort Lyon, patrolled and fought on both the

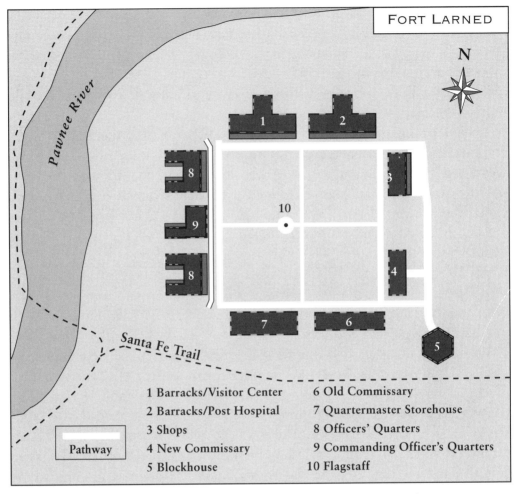

N

1 Barracks/Visitor Center   6 Old Commissary
2 Barracks/Post Hospital   7 Quartermaster Storehouse
3 Shops   8 Officers' Quarters
4 New Commissary   9 Commanding Officer's Quarters
5 Blockhouse   10 Flagstaff

Pathway

Fort Larned consisted of an open quadrangle surrounded by a small collection of unassuming buildings, unprotected by any stockade. Yet for nearly 40 years it served as a base for soldiers and cavalry protecting the Santa Fe Trail.

Mountain and Cimarron branches of the route. Originally constructed in 1859, it began as a small, makeshift fortification near Lookout Hill (now called Jenkins Hill) on the bank of the Pawnee River, about five miles from the river's junction with the Arkansas River. It was at first called simply the "Camp at Pawnee Fort." The name was soon changed, perhaps more appropriately, to "Camp Alert." When the installation was moved three miles west to its present location in 1860, it received its final name, Camp Larned, after Colonel Benjamin F. Larned, the U.S. Army paymaster general.

The 1860 buildings were constructed of sod and adobe, much to the displeasure of Captain Henry W. Wessells of the 2nd Infantry, who was in charge of the original construction. Wessells had wanted to use a cleaner and sturdier wood-and-stone construction, but had been ordered to build with adobe instead. Between 1866 and 1868, Wessells was proved right when all of the "shabby, vermin-breeding" original structures had to be torn down and replaced by the sandstone-and-wood buildings standing today.

Surrounding a 400-foot parade ground, the nine buildings and their interior rooms have been filled with accurate reproductions of all their original fixtures and fittings. The Barracks (two buildings), Officers' Quarters, Commanding Officer's Quarters, Quartermaster Storehouse, Old Commissary, New Commissary, Shops Building, and Blockhouse make up the fort, and all are open for display.

Parade grounds at Fort Larned (Courtesy of the National Park Service)

To the soldiers stationed at Larned, the Barracks, each holding two companies of men, were the heart of the fort. Each company was allotted five rooms: a squad room where the men slept two to a bunk and head to toe; an orderly room where the first sergeant and commissary sergeant slept and kept their daily records; a mess hall; a kitchen; and a pantry for food storage. The cooking was done on a large woodstove and the meals were basic. Hash, stew, bread, salt pork, and beans were all standard items. Fresh meat usually came from slaughtered beef and occasionally from buffalo. Although each company had its own cook and mess, there was never an "official" cook—cooks were selected from the ranks, usually on a turn-by-turn basis.

Since Fort Larned was primarily a base of operations and not a true fortification, troops were constantly changing and being shuttled to and from the fort as they were needed at various points of trouble on the Plains. Between 1867 and 1869, Larned was the base of Company A of the 10th Cavalry, the first unit of Buffalo Soldiers to be assigned field duty. Nicknamed Buffalo Soldiers by the Native American tribes because of their courage in battle, the 10th Cavalry's two-year stay at Fort Larned ended in brutal tragedy fueled by senseless prejudice. The African-American soldiers compiled an excellent record during the years they patrolled the Santa Fe Trail, engaging in many major skirmishes with attacking Native American warriors. They also had the lowest desertion record and the least incidence of alcoholism in the entire army. And yet, they often met with racial prejudice in the camps. Fort Larned, unfortunately, was no exception. Repeated harassment and continual insults heaped upon the black soldiers finally led to an incident in which the 10th Cavalry's stables caught fire and burned in the early morning of January 2, 1869. Arson was strongly suspected, and 39 horses died in the flames. A race riot would certainly have broken out, averted only when the post commander quickly dispatched the proud and justifiably angered Buffalo Soldiers to another fort.

Commanding officers changed almost as often as troops at Fort Larned, and during its two decades of operation, the fort was commanded by 40 different officers, several of whom served more than once. You can visit the Commanding Officer's Quarters today—a two-story structure and the only single-family residence on the post. It contains four large rooms separated by a central hallway, a kitchen, and an upstairs dining quarters. Like the other structures in the fort, it is furnished in the style and taste of its time.

Flanking the post commander's house on each side are the subordinate officers' quarters. These two identical buildings are each one story high and shaped in the form of a rectangle. Each of the buildings housed two captains and four lieutenants. The captains' quarters at each end of the buildings were made up of four rooms—two for the captains' use, a kitchen, and a servant's room. The lieutenants had one room each without kitchens. In 1870 small wooden lean-tos were added to the rear to provide kitchens and servants' quarters.

The food supplies for the officers and men were distributed from the Old Commissary, the oldest surviving structure in the fort. Located next to the Quartermaster's Storehouse, the Old Commissary for many years also housed an arsenal and powder magazine in its western end. The adjacent Quartermaster's Storehouse acted as the supply center for the fort, and the building's large, open storeroom was filled with military clothing, bedding, tents, field gear, tools, and other materials needed to carry out frontier military missions.

Built to house the overflow of food and supplies, the New Commissary, located at a right angle from the Old Commissary, also served for a while as a hospital annex. In 1871 the north end was used as a library and schoolroom for the children on the post. The Shops Building, located to the right of the New Commissary (when you are facing the 100-foot flagstaff in the center of the Parade Grounds), housed a bakery and blacksmith's forge at either end, while the center area was used by carpenters, wheelwrights, painters, tinsmiths, and saddlers.

Perhaps the most striking feature for first-time visitors to Fort Larned today is the shocking absence of one particular feature—there is no stockade or wall around the perimeter of the post. It sits open and apparently defenseless on the wide Kansas plain. While a few of the buildings have rifle slits in their walls, the fort offers little in the way of actual protection from attack. Economy was one reason. Kansas in the 1860s was still very much a true prairie and a vast, treeless expanse. Shipping enough lumber in to build a logs-on-end stockade was prohibitively expensive in the eyes of the War Department. The second, and perhaps most important, reason was the nature of warfare employed by the Plains Indians. The Plains warrior was a master

Rangers dressed in U.S. cavalry uniforms stop to talk in the hot Kansas sun. (Courtesy of the National Park Service)

of hit-and-run tactics and guerrilla warfare, and was not interested in siege warfare and disastrous high-casuality battles. Large numbers of whooping and hollering warriors simply did not circle around a fort as happens so often in Hollywood movies.

The Indian Wars wound down in the late 1860s, following a victory by Lt. Col. George Armstrong Custer and his 7th Cavalry over Black Kettle's Cheyenne at the Battle of the Washita on November 27, 1868. Fort Larned then moved into its last period of operation. Ironically its last important function was to end the usefulness of the trail it had been set up to protect. With the end of the Civil War and the first early stirrings of the Industrial Revolution, the railroads began to surge across the western plains. In the early 1870s, as the Santa Fe Railroad pushed west from Topeka, soldiers from Fort Larned were assigned to protect the track layers and construction workers. By July 1878, six years after the completion of the railroad, the old Santa Fe Trail became less and less heavily traveled because railway travel made the journey so much safer, faster, and cheaper. Fort Larned was effectively abandoned as an active military post, with only a small guard of soldiers on hand to protect the property.

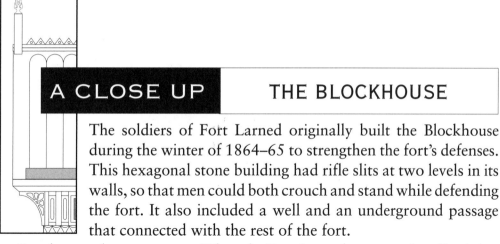

A CLOSE UP · THE BLOCKHOUSE

The soldiers of Fort Larned originally built the Blockhouse during the winter of 1864–65 to strengthen the fort's defenses. This hexagonal stone building had rifle slits at two levels in its walls, so that men could both crouch and stand while defending the fort. It also included a well and an underground passage that connected with the rest of the fort.

But the attacks never came. When the Fort Larned command realized that they didn't need the structure for defense, the soldiers put the building to use as a clothing storehouse and arsenal for a few years, and later it became a guardhouse to imprison unruly soldiers.

Soldiers sent to the guardhouse usually received orders to bring their own blankets for protection against the bitter cold of the Kansas plains—the building lacked such luxuries as a wooden floor or a stove. While the imprisoned soldiers would spend their nights in the structure, they generally didn't spend their days there. Instead, they received assignments to perform such unpleasant chores as cleaning up the outhouses.

The reconstructed blockhouse, as viewed from across the parade grounds   (Courtesy of the
National Park Service)

Sometime after the fort was sold to civilian owners, they tore down the
original Blockhouse and used its sandstone blocks for other purposes. The
only completely rebuilt structure in the fort, the Blockhouse was returned to
its original position by the National Park Service.

PRESERVING IT FOR THE FUTURE

On March 26, 1883, the Fort Larned Military Reservation was transferred
from the War Department to the General Land Office, U.S. Department of
the Interior. A year later the buildings and land were sold at public auction,

and for the next 80 years the property remained in private hands. In August 1964, Fort Larned became a National Historic Site and a unit of the National Park System. Since that time the National Park Service has begun to restore the existing buildings to appear as they did in 1868, with the exception of the East Barracks, which will include the hospital added after 1871. The restored fort, with its authentic museum exhibits and living history interpretations, brings to life the turbulent era of the westward movement and the conflict between an expanding nation and the Plains Indians.

The Santa Fe Trail became a National Historic Trail in 1987.

EXPLORING ♦ FURTHER

Books about Westward Trails, and the Soldiers Who Defended Them

Cox, Clinton. *The Forgotten Heroes: The Story of the Buffalo Soldiers*. New York: Scholastic, 1993.

Gibbon, General John. *Adventures on the Western Frontier*. Edited by Alan Gaff and Maureen Gaff. Bloomington: Indiana University Press, 1994.

Reef, Catherine. *Buffalo Soldiers*. New York: Twenty-First Century Books, 1993.

Simmons, Marc, editor. *On the Santa Fe Trail*. Lawrence: University Press of Kansas, 1986.

Utley, Robert Marshall. *Fort Larned National Historic Site*. Tucson, Ariz.: Southwest Parks and Monuments Association, 1993.

Wadsworth, Ginger. *Along the Santa Fe Trail: Marion Russell's Own Story*, by Marion Russell; adapted by Ginger Wadsworth; illustrated by James Watling. Morton Grove, Ill.: A. Whitman, 1993.

Yount, Lisa. *Frontier of Freedom: African Americans in the West*. New York: Facts On File, 1997. Has a chapter on the Buffalo Soldiers.

Related Places

Fort Davis National Historic Site
P.O. Box 1456
Highways 17–118

Fort Davis, TX 79734
(915) 426-3224
Fax: (915) 426-3122

Soldiers from this West Texas post played an important role in opening the area to settlement, protecting travelers and merchants along the San Antonio–El Paso Road from 1854 to 1891. Many consider the fort the best preserved in the Southwest. The 460-acre site was authorized as a National Historic Site on September 8, 1961, and established on July 4, 1963.

Fort Bowie National Historic Site
Bowie, AZ
Write c/o Superintendent, Chiricahua National Monument
Dos Cabezas Route Box 6500
Willcox, AZ 85643
(520) 847-2500

In its 1,000 acres, Fort Bowie stands as a symbol of the bitter conflict between the Chiricahua Apache and the U.S. military that lasted for more than 30 years. Fort Bowie and Apache Pass became the focal point of a struggle that finally ended in the surrender of Geronimo in 1886 and the exile of the Chiricahua to Florida and Alabama. A wagon train massacre known as the Bascom Affair took place here, and a large force of Chiricahua Apache under Mangas Coloradas and Cochise fought the California Volunteers in the Battle of Apache Pass.

The remains of Fort Bowie are now carefully preserved. The adobe walls of various post buildings and the ruins of the Butterfield Stage Station are still standing. And the fort remains as a lasting memorial to the bravery and endurance of U.S. soldiers who helped families move to new homes and hopeful travelers seek new lives in the West. It also serves to remind us of the painful "clash of two cultures," one a young emerging nation in pursuit of its "manifest destiny," the other a valiant hunter-gatherer society fighting to preserve its existence. Apache resistance was finally crushed at Fort Bowie, and the result was the end of the Indian Wars in the southwest United States.

Bodie State Historic Park

GOLD RUSH GHOST TOWN
Bodie, California

AT A GLANCE

Built: 1859

W. S. Body, a prospector, discovered gold here in 1859. Today about 150 buildings remain of the once-prosperous town that sprang up, now one of the best preserved ghost towns in the United States.

Only about 5 percent of the buildings that once lined the streets of Bodie still remain. In its heyday—about 1880—it was the scene of raucous jubilance, desperation, and the wild spirit of gold fever. Today, it stands just as time, fire, and the weather have left it, in a state of arrested decay.

Address:
Bodie State Historic Park
P.O. Box 515
Bridgeport, CA 93517
(760) 647-6445

> *Once a town of 10,000 people, today only tumbleweeds scuttle through the streets of Bodie, along with an occasional tourist. It is a town without a population.*

Good-bye God, I'm going to Bodie.

—Entry in a girl's diary

♦ ♦ ♦ ♦ ♦

There's something haunting and unnatural about an abandoned house. A house filled with people is normal. It is fulfilling its function—housing life, activity, the human sounds of women, men, and children, their cries and laughter, their hopes, dreams, and disappointments. Even a temporarily empty house—one in transition from one set of human inhabitants to the next—still retains the warmth of its last residents. It is simply and undramatically waiting, assured of its future occupants. An abandoned house, though, is both dead and undead. A ghost. A haunted, empty shell, its warmth turned cold, its memories locked forever in time, its function condemned ever to a kind of purgatory—it stands waiting, brooding, a reminder only of its past, forever without a future.

Sometimes such a fate awaits entire towns.

The ghost town of Bodie, California, sits quietly in a natural basin, surrounded by hills in the high desert country of eastern California. Down its deserted streets the warm desert winds turn cold at night, rattling an occasional loose board or shingle, blowing dead sagebrush between the empty rows of houses.

Once, one of the West's wildest towns stood here, filling these same streets, these same houses, with human life. So much life in fact that it could not contain itself within restrictions, and so much human energy that it burst at the seams of conventionality, sprawling forth—wild, noisy, and dangerous—into legend.

At the time, the Reverend F. M. Warrington spoke for many respectable people when he called the town "a sea of sin, lashed by the tempests of lust and passion." The townspeople of Bodie laughed and went about their business. The business of Bodie was gold, finding it, mining it, and spending the wages of its concern on whatever pleasure the human mind could devise when the long hard workday was through. At one point, near its peak of activity in 1880, Bodie's main streets were home to 65 saloons. Over 10,000 people walked those streets, and nearly 2,000 buildings spread over the townsite and the surrounding hills. It was a boomtown, brought about in a rush of gold, kept alive briefly by gold, and dying when the gold played out.

The town was named after Waterman S. Body, also known as William S. Bodey, who had discovered gold nearby in 1859. At some point the good citizens had changed the spelling from Body to Bodie to ensure that the town's name would be pronounced correctly. It was a good decision. Body may have hit a little too close to home and frightened other newcomers, such as the anonymous little girl who, upon hearing that her parents intended to move to the notorious town, wrote in her diary, "Good-bye God, I'm going to

View of Bodie from Standard Hill, showing the intersection of Green Street (lower left to upper right) and Main Street (lower right to upper left) (Courtesy of the Bodie State Historic Park)

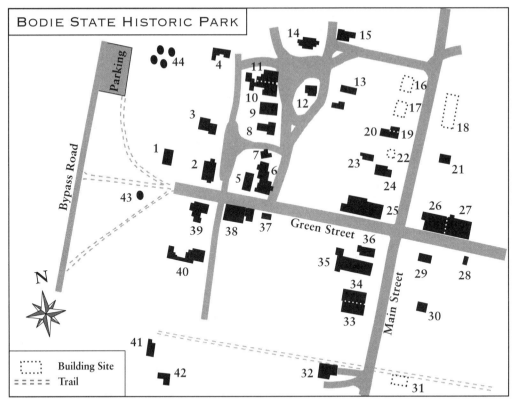

BODIE STATE HISTORIC PARK

Parking

Bypass Road

N

Building Site

Trail

Green Street

Main Street

Once a sprawling town of over 10,000 people, Bodie's buildings now stand vacant and abandoned, housing only memories of the vivid history that took place here.

Bodie." Killings in the streets, saloons, and pleasure palaces were a common thing during Bodie's brief life. At one point the town averaged nearly one homicide a day and during burials the residents had taken to tolling the firehouse bell once for each year of the victim's age. The bells were seldom still.

Although Bodie had first come into existence in 1859, it wasn't until 1865 —when prospectors discovered a rich vein of gold—that its boom period began. The population peaked in 1880 when over 30 full-scale mining companies were working in the area. But by 1882 much of the gold was already gone, and by 1884 the town was for all practical purposes dead. Death came so quickly that many of the townspeople simply abandoned their household goods, and even storekeepers left with merchandise still lining their shelves. With the gold gone there was no reason to stay, and with winter

1 Dolan House   2 The old Methodist Church, originally erected in 1882   3 Home of Dan McDonald, who was injured in 1879 in an early use of dynamite at the Standard works   4 Home of Henry Metzger, foreman of the Standard Mill   5 Tom Miller House (open to the public). Tom Miller worked for the Mono Lake Railway and Lumber Company   6 Residence of James Stuart Cain, a major Bodie property owner, and his wife, Martha. The Park Office is located here   7 Sawmill, used for cutting firewood for Bodie's long, cold winters   8 Donnelly House. Originally the home of town butcher Charlie Donnelly, who married English artist Annie Pagdin   9 Seiler House, home of a Bodie saloonkeeper   10 Cameron House, later a residence of Martha and James Stuart Cain   11 Home of Lester Bell, who ran the cyanide plant, which played a key role in extracting gold from mine tailings (waste products)   12 Mendocini house, once occupied by Annie Mendocini, whose father drove freight wagons   13 Home of M. J. Cody, U.S. Land Agent, 1885–86   14 House of Pat Reddy, criminal lawyer and defender of labor union members   15 Murphy House   16 Site of the Sawdust Corner Saloon   17 Site of Soderling Assay Office   18 Site of the Occidental Hotel, where the ruins of the hotel's stone warehouse are still visible   19 Barber shop   20 Sam Leon Bar   21 Firehouse   22 The carpenter shop, which collapsed in the winter of 1973–74   23 Fulton's Stable   24 Home of Lottie Johl, who began her career in the red-light district but later became a successful painter   25 Boone Store and Warehouse, erected in 1879   26 Wheaton & Hollis Hotel and Bodie Store   27 The Hydroelectric Building and Power Substation   28 Kelley House   29 The Swazey Hotel, which also served at various times as a clothing store and casino   30 Old barn   31 Site of bottle works   32 County barn   33 Dechambeau Hotel. In 1879 this building housed the Post Office, later Grandma Johnson's rooming house, and finally the Dechambeau Hotel   34 I.O.O.F. Hall. Oddfellows Lodge #279 (Independent Order of Odd Fellows) used the upper floor of this building   35 Miners' Union Hall (and Museum/Visitor Center). Built in 1878, this was the heart of social life in Bodie. The building now houses a museum   36 Morgue (where caskets can still be seen through the windows)   37 Boone Granary   38 Old red barn   39 D. V. Cain House, built in 1873   40 Sturgeon House   41 Home of William L. Brown, who earned $1.00 a day as a miner around 1930 (compared to $4.00 a day earned by union miners during the boom days of the 19th century)   42 Moyle House. The Moyle brothers were merchants, and George Moyle later owned the bottling plant (#31) and played on the Bodie baseball team   43 Machinery, including a generator once belonging to the Bodie hydroelectric power plant   44 Headframe (sometimes called a "gallows frame"), once used for hoisting at the Red Cloud Mine. Also on view here, the Red Cloud's steam hoist and air compressor

coming on—temperatures often dropped to 20–40°F below zero and snow-drifts piled as high as 20 feet in the streets—there was good reason not to tarry.

Today some 150 buildings still stand witness to Bodie's historic past. Designated a State Historic Park in 1962, the town of Bodie remains in a state of "arrested decay." It is neither being restored nor allowed to fall to the ground. Although some walls and roofs have been propped up to keep them from collapsing, there is no repainting, rebuilding, or restructuring going on in Bodie. If ghosts did indeed exist, it would be in Bodie that they would most comfortably roam. Unlike many other ghost towns scattered across the west there is no commercialization of Bodie. You can't buy trinkets, souvenirs, food, or drink in its streets. Even film for cameras is dispensed in only very small quantities at the park center lodged in the old Miner's Union

Hall building. Toilets are in the parking lot outside the town. There are no gas stations, camping grounds, or lodging facilities in the area. Although the town is open year round, the park department advises visitors to use snowmobiles, snowshoes, or skis to get to the site in the winter months. Even four-wheel-drive vehicles find the going too rough and often get stuck in the deep snow that blankets the entire area.

What you can do in Bodie is walk through the past. History will not be reenacted by actors in colorful costumes, but will unfold in your own mind as you walk the dusty streets, enter some of the open buildings, and peek into the windows of deserted houses. The smell of old decayed wood and dust fills the air. Old mining equipment rusts silently amid the sagebrush, and sand gathers around the broken wheels of an occasional wagon still standing in the streets. You can visit the town jail, badly in disrepair now, but once airtight. Bail for all prisoners was $5, and no one was ever known to escape —although one prisoner was kidnapped by vigilantes and hanged. You can see the Boone Store and Warehouse, once owned by Harvey Boone, a direct descendent of Daniel Boone and a lover of fine horses. Harvey, one of the more "upscale" of the town's businessmen, protected his building with an ingenious form of siding—he used empty five-gallon kerosene cans, once used to light lanterns in the town, cutting them open and flattening them out into panels. Much of this siding is still intact. Looking through the building's windows you can see many of the shelves still stocked with the favored goods of the day.

Walking the streets, you can see the old firehouse, the post office, hotels, livery stables and warehouses, an undertaker's parlor with coffins still on display in its windows, and dozens of private homes and public buildings. You can see the Old Methodist Church, the only church still standing in Bodie, its pews still intact and in place. Also, still standing as representative of Bodie's more "respectable" past is the Bodie Schoolhouse. (It is actually the second Bodie schoolhouse; the first was burned down by a small boy who had gotten in trouble and had been sent home.) Inside the schoolhouse you can see the original desks, books, slate blackboards, and even a few toys, all left behind when the town was so hastily deserted.

Many other artifacts can be seen in the small museum set aside in the old Miner's Union Hall, where much of the town's "respectable" night life occurred, including an annual Fourth of July Grand Ball, Christmas parties,

Main Street in winter. Buildings left to right: Old post office, IOOF Hall, Miner's Union, morgue, and, across the intersection, the Boone Store (Courtesy of the Bodie State Historic Park)

and a much anticipated masquerade ball on George Washington's birthday. Safely housed in small glass cases, among many other items, is a wooden abacus, probably used by one of the town's storekeepers. There are Chinese books and coins, from the Chinatown section of Bodie, which you can also visit (although unfortunately not much stands now of what had once been a thriving "town within a town," complete with its own stores, gambling houses, saloons, and an opium den used by Caucasian and Chinese alike). Other items in the museum include such everyday tools as a hair-curling iron, pencil sharpeners used in the school and stores, a few children's toys, a pair of snowshoes, which look more like modern skis, and even a snowshoe for a horse—a metal plate about one foot square with a leather strap to hold it on the horse's hoof. The small museum is a momentarily quiet reminder that even in the wildest of Wild West towns, there were those who went about their business quietly and conscientiously, avoiding the town's sensations and helping to keep it running as smoothly as possible in the midst of its less savory hustle and bustle.

But Bodie was not known for its "respectable" side. How respectable could a town be that at one point had seven breweries working day and night, and had whiskey brought in regularly by horse carriage, one hundred barrels a load. Even in the lawless West, Bodie was notorious for its robberies, stagecoach holdups, beatings, and shootings. Today much of Bodie's less respectable past also stands—including badly deteriorating saloons, brothels, and gambling dens. Not all are easily recognized from their exterior appearance, but booklets available at the park station identify them street by street for the visitor.

Another reminder of the town's wild and wooly days can be seen just at the edge of town. Just outside the fence of the local cemetery, which you can also visit, is Boot Hill—the last stop for many of Bodie's hard cases. In the official cemetery some headstones of stone or wood are still standing though

Inside the Boone Store on Main Street (Courtesy of the Bodie State Historic Park)

many have fallen or been destroyed by vandals. There are no markers in Boot Hill, however—here the permanent "guests" were usually deposited without fanfare or headstone.

During the town's heyday there was a common legend in the West about a notorious character known as the "Badman from Bodie." Although some historians think he was an actual person, others believe it is more likely that the reference was merely symbolic of the town and its wild spirit.

Today that spirit still lingers in the buildings lining Bodie's dusty streets.

Moving quietly down those streets, or peering into the windows of its old buildings, you sometimes think that you hear a noise or catch a strange shadow flitting in the corner of a room or in an alleyway between the houses. But then, what is a ghost town without the presence of ghosts—images of the past, haunting the minds of the present.

Few places in the West allow those ghosts to roam as freely as they do in Bodie.

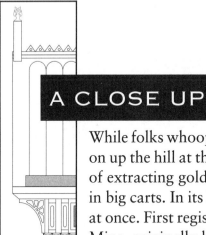

A CLOSE UP — THE STANDARD MINE STAMP MILL

While folks whooped it up in town, the business of mining went on up the hill at the mines. Stamp mills mechanized the process of extracting gold from the rock ore brought in by the miners in big carts. In its heyday, Bodie had eight stamp mills running at once. First registered in 1861, the stamp mill at the Standard Mine, originally known as the Bunker Hill Mine, now stands quiet, but most of its inner workings are still intact.

You can't just wander through this area of Bodie, for safety reasons, but scheduled guided tours of the stamp mill take place during the summer months, and special guided tours for groups of 20 or less can be arranged in the spring and fall.

Firehouse, with the Standard Mine Stamp Mill in the background (Courtesy of the Bodie State Historic Park)

Steam engines powered the mills and hoisting works at the mines, and it took large amounts of wood to generate the steam power. But wood was scarce in the area around Bodie, so most of the firewood had to be shipped in. In 1881 a 33-mile, narrow-gauge railroad was constructed to bring wood in from a lumber mill located at Mono Lake. This system continued in use until 1917, after which the track and most of the ties were removed (and probably fed to the belching steam engine of the mill).

Electricity came into use at the mill in 1892—it was transmitted from a hydroelectric plant on Green Creek, 13 miles away, a major distance for that time. This was among the first successful long-distance transmissions of alternating current in the United States.

When the mill was in full operation, it took 14 men to operate the machinery, which combined the use of gravity and moving belts to feed ore from the cars into a series of sorters and crushing mechanisms. First the ore passed through large steel grates, called grizzlies, that sorted the chunks by size. Then it moved on to the big Blake crusher, which used powerful mechanical jaws to break up the ore. The ore then passed through another grizzly and moved on to the heart of the mill: the stamps.

Here the ore was pulverized into a powder by the rising and falling of the heavy, pistonlike stamps. Afterward, the powdered ore was mixed with water to form an ore soup, called a slurry, which flowed out of the stamp battery and onto the amalgamation tables. These were surfaces sheathed in copper and coated with mercury. As the slurry flowed over the tables, the tiny particles of gold and silver adhered to the mercury in a process called amalgamation. From there, the slurry flowed onto concentrator tables, where it was washed with water and shaken, just in case any additional gold or silver particles had escaped being captured by the mercury.

This stamp mill alone processed more than $14 million worth of gold in 25 years, and over the life of Bodie, more than $100 million was taken out of the gold mines—an enormous amount of money at that time, and not a bad take even today. But by 1938 the boom had long since ended and this once-active mill ground and pounded metal from rock for the last time. Today, its muteness contributes to the eerie stillness of Bodie.

PRESERVING IT FOR THE FUTURE

In 1962 the ghost town of Bodie, California, became a state historic park, established to preserve, protect, and interpret its history and legacy. Today this Old West mining town is maintained in a state of "arrested decay." That is, the park system's policy is neither to restore it, nor to let it fall to the ground. Visitors can wander through its empty streets, peer through the windows of some 150 remaining structures, and imagine what it must have been like when times were prosperous. The park comprises some 500 acres, situated in a small valley at 8,375 feet above sea level. It is the only California State Park representing the high desert mountain landscape in the Great Basin region, and the surrounding area contains unique plant and animal life, climatic conditions, and geology, in addition to the cultural heritage it protects. The Friends of Bodie, a nonprofit volunteer group dedicated to the preservation of the once gold-rich ghost town, takes an active part in providing financial support and volunteers.

EXPLORING ♦ FURTHER

Books about Bodie and the Gold Rush

Blake, Arthur, and Pamela Dailey. *The Gold Rush of 1849: Staking a Claim in California*. (Spotlight on American History) Brookfield, Conn.: Millbrook Press, 1995.

Kaufman, Polly Welts, editor. *Apron Full of Gold: The Letters of Mary Jane Megquier from San Francisco, 1849–1856*. 2nd Edition. Albuquerque: University of New Mexico Press, 1994.

Rohrburg, Malcolm J. *Days of Gold: The California Gold Rush and the American Nation*. Berkeley: University of California Press, 1997.

Stein, R. Conrad. *The California Gold Rush*. (Cornerstones of Freedom) Revised Edition. Chicago: Childrens Press, 1995.

Van Steenwyk, Elizabeth. *The California Gold Rush: West with the Forty-Niners*. (A First Book) New York: Franklin Watts, 1991.

Wedertz, Frank. *Bodie, 1859–1900*. Bishop, Calif.: Chalfont Press, 1969.

Related Places

Donner Memorial State Park
12593 Donner Pass Road
Truckee, CA 96161
(916) 582-7892

In 1846 a great westward movement began; and in April 1846 a loose-knit band of midwestern farmers and adventurers left Independence, Missouri to travel west together. They set out across the Great Plains, crossing the Rocky Mountain range at South Pass, in Wyoming Territory, and then headed southwest through a relatively new and unexplored shortcut, or "cutoff." This cutoff turned out to be anything but a shortcut, adding several weeks to their travel time—weeks they could not afford. The party finally reached present-day Truckee in late October, 1846. It was too late. Already starving, their stamina depleted, the travelers encountered in this high, isolated valley one of the earliest and most severe of Sierra winters. They could not climb out of the Truckee Basin, and they were forced to remain there to wait out the winter. In January 1847 a few of the group succeeded in climbing the 7,088-foot pass (now Donner Pass), and they summoned relief parties. By April 1847 only 48 of the 89 emigrants who comprised the Donner Party were still alive. Nearly half, 41 in all, had died along the way, most of them starving or freezing. The 48 survivors had subsisted on their few meager provisions, ox hides, which ran out all too soon, and finally the bodies of their dead friends and relatives. No more tragic and gruesome story exists in the saga of the American West. Donner Memorial State Park is now located where many of the emigrants, now known as the Donner Party, spent their last days. A huge monument now stands where they built one of their cabins; its base is 22 feet high, reminding visitors how deep the snow piled up during that winter of 1846–47. Others who traveled through the Truckee area in emigrant trains were not so unlucky later that year, in the summer and fall of 1847. And in January 1848, James Marshall discovered gold at Sutter's Mill near Coloma in the Sierra foothills. Word spread quickly, and the great California gold rush was on.

Marshall Gold Discovery State Historic Park
Gold Discovery Park Association
P.O. Box 265
310 Back Street
Coloma, CA 95613
(916) 622-3470 or 622-6198

This is where the California gold rush began in January 1848, when James Marshall discovered gold at Sutter's Mill. A full-sized replica of Sutter's Mill provides one of the park's main attractions. Although the original was abandoned and vandalized, and finally disappeared completely in floods of the 1850s, the replica represents a close approximation of the original, based on extensive research. It was completed in 1968 and operates regularly to the delight of park visitors. Some of the original mill's timbers were reclaimed from the river and are displayed nearby, and other exhibits throughout the park display artifacts connected with mining for gold.

Fruita Orchards

RURAL PIONEER VILLAGE
Capitol Reef National Park, Utah

AT A GLANCE

Founded ca. 1879

A pioneer community settled in the 1880s, this remote village was home until 1969 to about 10 families at a time, supported by the orchards planted by the early settlers.

Fruita's orchards include about 2,700 trees and are composed of cherry, apricot, peach, pear, and apple. A few plum, mulberry, almond, and walnut trees also grow here. Fruita is now located inside the Capitol Reef National Park, Utah. The park is made up of some 241,904 acres (378 square miles).

Address:
Capitol Reef National Park
HC 70, Box 15
Torrey, UT 84775-9602
(801) 425-3791, Ext.111
http://www.nps.gov/care/

Remotely located in the rugged terrain of Utah, this tiny community built its economy on the fruit orchards planted by the first settlers. Insulated from outside influences, Fruita was able to survive the Great Depression of the 1930s, only to dissolve once modern roads brought the rest of the world to its doorstep. Today, only the fruit trees remain.

. . . A sudden, intensely green little valley among the cliffs of the Waterpocket Fold, opulent with cherries, peaches, and apples in season, inhabited by a few families who were about equally good Mormons and good frontiersmen and good farmers . . .

—Wallace and Page Stegner,
American Places

♦ ♦ ♦ ♦ ♦

An eroded mass of colorful cliffs and rocky, twisting canyons make up the Waterpocket Fold, a 100-mile-long wrinkle in the earth's crust that stretches across south-central Utah. It is a place of cactus, juniper, and columbine, of jackrabbits, lizards, jays, and deer. The Fremont River meanders on a twisting path in the Fold, and where the river meets up with Sulphur Creek, you find the tiny settlement of Fruita, hugging the banks today just as it did in the 1880s, when it was first settled by Mormon pioneers.

Settlement from the east came relatively late to rugged south-central Utah, but Native Americans had been in this craggy wilderness area for a long time before the first rough-hewn cabin of an early pioneer went up. The Fremont and Anasazi Indians had first occupied the Fold and later the Paiute and Ute—and perhaps, as some evidence suggests, also the Navajo.

No one knows for certain who the first white settler was, but it may have been a squatter by the name of Franklin Young who was known to have been around the area in 1879. The first official landowner, according to the records, was a man named Nels Johnson. A few others soon followed and the tiny Mormon community that sprang up along the banks of the river became known as Junction. Driven west by opposition to their religious beliefs, the Mormons had settled and founded Salt Lake City, Utah, in 1847, but the Waterpocket Fold area hadn't even been charted by dependable explorers until 1871. What drew the first Mormons into the Fold isn't known, but their reason for staying was the potential for planting orchards that could be fed by the meandering Fremont River. The orchards soon prospered, and by the turn of the century Junction was known as "the Eden of Wayne County." In 1900, perhaps to give the tiny community greater identification with its primary reason for being, the residents changed the settlement's name to Fruita.

Although the orchards prospered, and remain one of the settlement's primary attractions today, Fruita never really grew very large. Even at its peak, around the time of World War I, the population averaged only around 10 families. It was just too isolated and off the beaten path to ever draw more. In 1883 the residents laboriously built a rough road through the

Nestled in this rough, rocky central Utah terrain, pioneer Fruita and its orchards formed a small, productive oasis in the desert. (Courtesy of the Salt Lake Convention and Visitors Bureau)

The waters of Sulphur Creek and the Fremont River watered the community's thirsty orchards.
(Courtesy of the Salt Lake Convention and Visitors Bureau)

narrow gorge to allow them access to the nearby towns of Cainsville and Hanksville. But the narrow, twisting roadway, called the Blue Dugway (after the gray blue shale deposits it cut through), was so difficult to travel that it often took more than an hour and a half for a horse and wagon to go 10 miles. Well into the mid-20th century Fruita remained one of the most isolated communities in America. Ironically, it was this very isolation that aided the settlement during the Great Depression of the 1930s. Since there was never very much outside travel into the community, cash had always been in short supply and barter was the main means for acquiring goods and services. The long established ritual shielded the Fremont River settlement from the cash shortage that devastated much of the rest of the nation. Isolation shielded the Fruita community during the depression, but when the isolation ended, so did the active life of the little community.

With the establishment of the 242,000-acre Capitol Reef National Monument by the National Park Service in 1937, the area was opened up to tourists from the outside world. New roads were built, old ones were paved, and the flow of visitors to the National Park that now surrounded Fruita increased almost daily. By the mid-1950s the outside world had so completely entered the Waterpocket Fold that the Park Service had begun purchasing land parcels from the Fruita residents. By the 1960s the people of Fruita had sold most of their private land to the Park Service, and many of the settlement's structures and outbuildings were torn down. The last resident, Dewey Gifford, who for a brief time worked for the Park Service, sold his home in 1969 and moved away, thus ending the history of the tiny Mormon settlement.

Today Fruita is part of the Capitol Reef National Monument, and most of Fruita's famous orchards are still thriving. Now completely owned by the U.S. government, the orchards are maintained at a level of about 2,500 trees with around 1,800 in production. A small Park Service crew works year round, pruning, irrigating, replanting, and spraying. Cherry, apricot, peach, pear, and apple as well as a few plum, mulberry, almond, and walnut trees make up the crop. Visitors are welcome to wander into any unlocked orchards and consume as much fruit as they like while in the orchards. Those who visit the orchards at dusk are very likely to see mule deer enjoying the downed fruit. During harvest time the fruit can be taken by the public on a "pick your own" basis. The Park superintendent sets the price per pound or per bushel after checking the prices in local commercial orchards, taking care not to sell for less and thus undercut the local commercial markets.

Roads built in the 1940s and 1950s brought a different kind of life to the region where Fruita survived—and brought the life of the community to an end. (Courtesy of the Salt Lake Convention and Visitors Bureau)

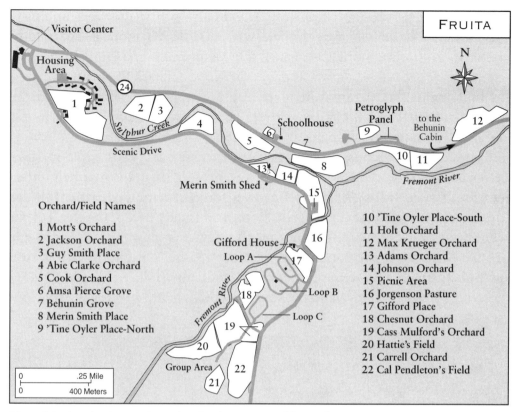

Visitor Center

Housing Area

24

Sulphur Creek

Scenic Drive

1

2 3

4

5

6 Schoolhouse 7

13 14

Merin Smith Shed

15

16

Gifford House

Loop A

17

Loop B

Loop C

18

19

20

21

22

Group Area

Fremont River

Petroglyph Panel 9 to the Behunin Cabin 12

10 11

Fremont River

8

N

Orchard/Field Names

1 Mott's Orchard
2 Jackson Orchard
3 Guy Smith Place
4 Abie Clarke Orchard
5 Cook Orchard
6 Amsa Pierce Grove
7 Behunin Grove
8 Merin Smith Place
9 'Tine Oyler Place-North

10 'Tine Oyler Place-South
11 Holt Orchard
12 Max Krueger Orchard
13 Adams Orchard
14 Johnson Orchard
15 Picnic Area
16 Jorgenson Pasture
17 Gifford Place
18 Chesnut Orchard
19 Cass Mulford's Orchard
20 Hattie's Field
21 Carrell Orchard
22 Cal Pendleton's Field

0   .25 Mile
0   400 Meters

Map of Fruita showing sections of orchards once owned by settlers

While in the area, visitors can also still see a few of the surviving structures of the Fruita settlement. Along the old Blue Dugway—vastly improved, it is now known as the Scenic Drive—they can find a few remainders of a way of life long since vanished in American history. The old Fruita Schoolhouse is a fine example. The small log building originally had a flat dirt-covered roof to shield it from the weather, but a peak shingled roof was added around 1912. The original walls, once of bare and chinked logs, were plastered in 1935. The desks were constructed of pine and seated two students each. Not bolted down, the desks could be moved aside for community functions like dances, town meetings, elections, or box-lunch socials. The school was built around 1892 on land donated by the Behunin family; and Nettie Behunin was the first teacher. Even though only eight families were living in the settlement at the time, they were large families, and Nettie's first class had 22 students. In 1900 the building was leased to the Wayne County School

District for the first county-approved classes and Nettie was kept on as the school's first authorized teacher. She was paid $70 a month. The school continued to operate until 1941 when there simply weren't enough students left in the area to fill the classes. In 1964 the National Park Service nominated the building to the National Register of Historic Places. They restored the structure to the way it looked in the 1930s, and that is the building that you can find today standing alongside Utah Highway 24 in Fruita.

The Behunin Cabin, where Nettie's family first lived for a while in 1882 before a flash flood destroyed their crops and forced them to move to another location, is also still standing and gives a forceful reminder of the spartan lifestyle of the early Fruita pioneers. Housing a family of ten, the small cabin with its single front window is not much larger than a present-day one-car garage. When the Behunin family lived here, the cabin's dirt floor was covered by braided rugs, and scraps of leftover dress materials served as window curtains. Although there was a fireplace for cooking and a water supply close

The barn on the old Gifford homestead, at the base of a rugged sandstone bluff (Courtesy of the National Park Service)

by, the family ate their meals outdoors. When night came the parents and the smallest children slept inside the cabin. The older girls slept outside in a bed made in an old wagon box, while the older boys slept in a dugout cut into the cliff above the cabin.

Larger, but still spartan, the Gifford Family Homestead (also still standing) was the home of the last resident. It was originally constructed in 1908 by Calvin Pendleton, and the Pendleton family occupied the house for eight years before it became the home of the Jorgen Jorgensen family. The original house had a combined front room/kitchen, two small bedrooms downstairs, and two small bedrooms upstairs that were accessed by climbing an outside ladder. The Pendletons also built a barn and smokehouse nearby as well as rock walls, which you can still see near the house and on the mesa slopes behind it. After the Jorgensen family took over the house in 1916 it was then sold to Jorgen Jogensen's son-in-law, Dewey Gifford, in 1928. The Giffords lived in the home for 41 years before it was taken over by the Park Service. The Giffords added a kitchen in 1947 and the bathroom, utility room, and carport in 1954. Electricity was added in 1948.

Still standing too is the Merin Smith Shed and Blacksmith Shop built around 1925, and there are many other reminders of old Fruita. Near the Johnson Pioneer Cabin Site, where Nels Johnson built the first permanent structure in Fruita, are two gigantic cottonwood trees, about 125 years old. One of these served as an outdoor post office—a small collection of mailboxes were affixed to it and used by the mail carrier who trudged along the Blue Dugway into Fruita bringing news and communications from the outside world. Signs posted in many of the orchards, fields, and pastures give the names of Fruita residents who at one time or other occupied the various sites during the settlement's nearly 75 years of existence. Land changed hands many times throughout those years, and as the Park Service points out, only about 10 families at a time ever occupied this tiny and isolated western community.

Surviving for over four decades on the hard labor of its inhabitants, Fruita is gone today. But even with only a few buildings left to evoke its physical presence, its enduring memory remains in the still producing, abundant, and beautiful orchards that gave the community its well-earned name.

A CLOSE UP KEEPING THE FAMILY FED

Like the other settlers in Fruita, the Gifford family was of necessity self-sufficient when it came to putting food on the table. The Giffords raised dairy cows, hogs, and sheep, as well as chickens and ducks. A smokehouse out back was used to preserve the meat for the family's use and occasionally for sale. The family also cultivated a large garden, producing a variety of vegetables including beans, potatoes, squash, peas, lettuce, radishes, corn, and watermelons. They also harvested fruit from a couple of orchards they owned. The fruit and vegetables were preserved by bottling or drying, with the freshly bottled foods being stored in the cellar in front of the house and the dry goods, including potatoes, being kept in a root cellar in back of the house.

PRESERVING IT FOR THE FUTURE

Today, the orchards of Fruita are preserved and protected as a Rural Historic Landscape. The National Park Service now owns and maintains the Fruita orchards with a two-person orchard crew that prunes, irrigates, and manages the orchards. Visitors are welcome to pick and eat the fruit on the grounds, or buy it to take off the premises, as well as visit the Fruita Schoolhouse and other structures left by the families who lived here.

EXPLORING ♦ FURTHER

Books about Frontier Utah and the Mormon Settlers

Bernotas, Bob. *Brigham Young*. (Library of Biography) New York: Chelsea House, 1993.

Doubleday, Veronica. *Salt Lake City*. (Holy Cities) New York: Dillon Press, 1994.

Fox, Mary Virginia. *The Story of Women Who Shaped the West*. (Cornerstones of Freedom) Chicago: Childrens Press, 1991.

Houk, Rose. *Capitol Reef: Canyon Country Eden*. Torrey, Utah: Capitol Reef Natural History Association, 1996.

Kinkead, Joyce A., editor. *A Schoolmarm All My Life: Personal Narratives from Frontier Utah*. Salt Lake City, Utah: Signature Books, 1996.

Roylance, Ward Jay. *Seeing Capitol Reef National Park: A Guide to the Roads and Trails*. Salt Lake City, Utah: Wasatch Publishers, 1979.

Sanford, William R. *Brigham Young: Pioneer and Mormon Leader*. (Legendary Heroes of the Wild West) Springfield, N.J.: Enslow Publishers, 1996.

Stegner, Wallace Earle. *Mormon Country. Second Edition*. Lincoln: University of Nebraska Press, 1982.

Related Place

Capitol Reef National Park
Petroglyph Pullout
HC 70, Box 15
Torrey, UT 84775-9602
(801) 425-3791, ext.111
http://www.nps.gov/care/

From this road pullout in Capitol Reef National Park, visitors can take an easy hike to see the earliest traces of human activity in this region—they were left by a group of people known by archaeologists as the Fremont Culture and date from the eighth century. The Fremont people left behind many petroglyphs, probably created between 700 and 1275, a large number of which have weathered the elements along this cliff. Apparently related to the Four Corners Anasazi people, but less sophisticated, the Fremont Indians suddenly abandoned their settlements and fields in the 13th century. No explanation for their demise has ever been found.

MORE PLACES TO VISIT

The chapters of this book explore only a few of the hundreds of historic sites that commemorate early settlements in America. Following is a partial list of additional historical places that explore the wide variety of types of settlements that helped make up what we know today as the United States.

New England

The Old Deerfield National Historic Landmark
Historic Deerfield, Inc.
Old Main Street
Deerfield, MA 01342
(413) 774-5581
Fax: (413) 773-7415
http://www.historic-deerfield.org

Originally settled in 1669 and resettled in 1707, this western Massachusetts village remains home to some 250 people, its population only slightly larger than it was in the 18th century. The original mile-long street settled in 1669 has been carefully preserved and protected and is now situated within the Old Deerfield National Historic Landmark. Each year thousands of visitors come to Deerfield to see the town's collection of 18th- and 19th-century houses, 14 of which are open to the public and display more than 20,000 objects made or used in America between 1650 and 1850. Many of the fall and winter scenes in the 1994 motion picture *Little Women* were filmed in Deerfield.

Hancock Shaker Village

P.O. Box 927
Pittsfield, MA 01202
(413) 443-0188 or (800) 817-1137
Fax: (413) 447-9357

Hancock Shaker Village, the Shakers' "City of Peace," recalls the way of life of one of America's most successful utopian societies. Refugees from religious persecution in their European homelands, the Shakers came to the United States seeking freedom to withdraw from society. Their doctrine called for independent, self-sufficient communities based on concepts of plain living, following the dictates of their conscience, and the practice of celibacy. Established in 1790, this village features 18 well-preserved buildings, including what may have been the first round barn in the United States. An active Shaker community from 1790 to 1960, the village now preserves the Shaker way of life in a living museum, where visitors can see and participate in Shaker life as it was in the 19th century.

Harrisville Historic District

Harrisville, NH 16038

Active from 1774 to 1900, this exceptionally well-preserved 19th-century industrial community includes a complex of mills, stores, boardinghouses, dwellings, churches, and other buildings—virtually intact and free from intrusions. About eight miles northwest of Peterborough, Harrisville's historic district still looks much as it did in the first half of the 1800s when it was a growing industrial community with mills that produced woolen cloth. The owners of Cheshire Mills built boardinghouses and single-family homes and rented them to the people who worked in the factories. With machine-cut lumber and nails readily available by 1866, houses like the ones found on Harrisville's Peanut Row could be quickly assembled. Workers rented these homes for $3 and $5 a week.

Old York Historical District

York Chamber of Commerce
P.O. Box 417

York, ME 03909
(207) 363-4422

York, founded in the early 1600s, is recognized as one of Maine's most historically significant communities. Old York is made up of seven historic sites, which together represent over 350 years of life in York. Maintained by the Old York Historical Society, the buildings include Jefferd's Tavern, a one-room Schoolhouse, the Elizabeth Perkins House, the Emerson-Wilcox House, the Old Gaol (this is the traditional British way of spelling "jail"), and, on the waterfront, the George Marshall Store and the John Hancock Warehouse (once owned by the colonial merchant and patriot John Hancock). As you pass through these buildings, you'll experience a little of what life was like in this seafaring town on the coast of Maine during the 18th and 19th centuries.

Atlantic Seaboard

Cape May National Historic Landmark
The Chamber of Commerce of Greater Cape May
P.O. Box 556
Cape May, NJ 08204
(609) 884-5508
Fax-on-demand: (609) 884-5508
E-mail: CCGCM@aol.com

Cape May was founded in 1620, the same year the Pilgrims landed at Plymouth, Massachusetts. When Dutch captain Cornelius Jacobsen Mey explored the Delaware River in this area, he named the peninsula that formed Delaware Bay after himself—the spelling later changed to Cape May. By 1761, a little over a century later, the town of Cape May had become the first seashore resort in America. But Cape May's most distinctive feature is its Victorian heritage, taken from a later era, which is apparent in the town's several hundred carefully preserved houses. During the years of Queen Victoria's reign in England (1837–1901), Cape May was considered to be among the top vacation resorts in the United States. Most of the town's homes, hotels, shops, and other buildings were constructed at the peak of the Victorian era. Today, the distinctive elements of Victorian architecture —carved bargeboards, ornate verandas, crowned dormers—have been restored. In 1976, Cape May became designated a National Historic Landmark City, one of only five in the nation.

Daniel Boone Homestead
500 Daniel Boone Road
Birdsboro, PA 19508
(610) 582-4900

Daniel Boone Homestead provides a unique glimpse of an early Pennsylvania settlement. Settled in 1730 by parents of the frontiersman Daniel Boone, the area was then sparsely populated by English, Quaker, German, Swiss, Huguenot, and Swedish pioneers. In this setting Daniel Boone was born (in 1734) and raised. Today, the historic site interprets not only the early life of the Boones but also the saga of the region's other settlers, comparing the lifestyles of different cultures in 18th-century rural Pennsylvania. The site includes the Boone house, a blacksmith's shop, a barn, the Bertolet log house, a sawmill, a Visitor Center, a picnic area, and trails. It is administered by the Pennsylvania Historical and Museum Commission.

Elfreth's Alley Historic District
Information: Elfreth's Alley Museum
126 Elfreth's Alley
Philadelphia, PA 19106
(215) 574-0560

Located off Second Street between Arch and Race Streets in Philadelphia, this narrow street dates back to the 18th and early 19th centuries. It is the oldest unchanged and continuously inhabited street in Philadelphia, illustrating city life in what was the largest city in colonial America. The houses on this street were built between 1720 and the early 1800s, many of them commissioned by Jeremiah Elfreth, a blacksmith and land speculator who built and rented out many of the alley's homes. Often he rented the homes to fellow artisans (such as cabinetmakers, silversmiths, pewterers, glassblowers, and wagon builders), local merchants, and tradesman of modest income. Their small houses were built side by side in rows, facing a narrow alleyway used for foot traffic and horse-drawn carts. Teachers and clergy also lived in Elfreth's Alley, often conducting business out of their homes. Each floor of these houses contained a single room, with a narrow, winding staircase connecting the floors. This type of house, known as a Trinity house, is very common in Philadelphia.

Ephrata Cloister
632 West Main Street
Ephrata, PA 17522
(717) 733-6600

The Ephrata Cloister was an 18th-century communal society rooted in religious mysticism. Best known for its original art and music, distinctive medieval German architecture, and publishing center, Ephrata Cloister was one of America's earliest communal societies. Housed in a collection of unique buildings, this community of religious celebrants practiced an austere lifestyle that placed spiritual and mystical goals above material objectives. Ten of the original buildings have been restored and interpreted to recreate this unusual communal site. Guides conducting the tours dress in the white habits used by the former inhabitants.

Old Economy Village
Ambridge, PA 15003
(412) 266-4500

This settlement was the third and final home of the Harmony Society, one of America's most successful 19th-century Christian communal groups, known for its piety and industrial prosperity. The original buildings, erected 1824–30, are furnished with objects belonging to the Harmonists, who came to Pennsylvania from Germany. They sought economic, religious, and social freedoms they could not find elsewhere. Seventeen carefully restored structures and gardens reflect their celibate lifestyle and an economic organization known worldwide primarily for its success in producing wool, cotton, and silk textiles. Their "cabinet of curiosities" and fine arts museum were first opened to the public in 1827. The site is administered by the Pennsylvania Historical and Museum Commission.

Fort Frederica National Monument

Route 9, Box 286-C
St. Simons Island, GA 31522-9710
(912) 638-3639
Fax: (912) 638-3639
http://www.nps.gov/fofr/

Founded in 1736, the town of Frederica was settled as the southernmost post to protect the British colonies in North America. The town formed around Fort Frederica, built on this island to protect Georgia and South Carolina from possible encroachment by the Spanish forces that had established colonies in Florida. The park is primarily an archaeological site, however, and no whole structures remain. But stately oaks, large grapevines and Spanish moss contribute to the sense of antiquity on the island, and the ruins of the old fort, including remants of the magazine barracks, along with foundations of the houses that once stood here, convey to visitors a sense of the day-to-day life of the old settlement.

Fort Raleigh National Historic Site

Roanoke Island, NC
Address: c/o Cape Hatteras National Seashore
Route 1, Box 675
Manteo, NC 27954
(919) 473-5772

The first English attempts at colonization in the New World (1585–87) are commemorated by this 513-acre National Historic Site on Roanoke Island. The colony, sponsored by Sir Walter Raleigh, came to a sudden end, however, with the disappearance of 116 men, women, and children (including two that were born in the New World). No one knows what happened to this "Lost Colony" and its fate remains a mystery to this day. Created in 1941, the park features a reconstruction of an earthen fort built by the English. An outdoor symphonic drama, *The Lost Colony*, has been performed here since 1937 in honor of the missing colonists.

Arkansas Post National Memorial

Rt. 1, Box 16
Gillett, AR 72055
(501) 548-2207

In 1686, Henri de Tonti established a trading post known as Poste de Arkansea at the Quapaw village of Osotuoy. It was the first semipermanent French settlement in the lower Mississippi River Valley. The establishment of the post was the first step in a long struggle between France, Spain, and England over the interior of the North American continent. The site of that trading post moved seven times during its history due to flooding from the Arkansas River.

Because of its strategic location near the point where the Arkansas River flows into the Mississippi, Arkansas Post made an ideal location for a fort, and both the French and later the Spanish located military installations there. In 1783 the Colbert Incident, the only Revolutionary War skirmish occurring west of the Mississippi, occurred at Arkansas Post. By 1819 the post was a thriving river port important enough to be selected the capital of the Arkansas Territory. In 1862, Confederate troops constructed an earthen fortification known as Fort Hindman. In January 1863, Union troops destroyed the fort and adjacent river port town, ensuring control of the Arkansas River.

Today, the park and museum commemorate the complex history of the site. Located on a peninsula bordered by the Arkansas River and two backwaters, the site offers excellent fishing and wildlife-watching opportunities. Visitors can view remnants of the historic town site, including a well, a cistern, and approximately 50 yards of Civil War earthworks from the Confederate defense lines.

Fort Snelling

Fort Snelling Historic Center
St. Paul, MN 55111
(612) 726-1171
At Minnesota Highways 5 and 55,
near the Twin Cities International Airport

Visitors to this 1827 stone fortress can talk with guides dressed as soldiers, cooks, laundresses, storekeepers, and craftspersons about life at this 1820s military outpost. Once at the edge of a small settlement, Fort Snelling is now at the center of Minnesota's Twin Cities metropolitan area. Built in 1820–24, this fort consists of 14 stone buildings and 2 log structures, erected on a site recommended by Zebulon Pike. It served as an important post on the edge of the European-American settlement in the Old Northwest. Today, costumed guides greet you as if you've just arrived via steamboat up the Mississippi River. The sights and sounds of the past fill the air as you hear musket fire, the cannon's roar, and the shrill tunes of the fife. Visitors are encouraged to join in by shouldering a musket, mending clothes, checking the stew, scraping a hide, or singing along with the soldiers. You can take tea with "Mrs. Snelling" or sample the soldiers' bread ration. Or you can swing a hammer in the blacksmith shop.

The fort was also later used as a troop training center during the Civil War, World War I, and World War II, and visitors can also explore the museum, which evokes these periods in its history.

Keweenaw National Historical Park
P.O. Box 471
Calumet, MI 49931
(800) 338-7982 (Keweenaw Tourism Council—for general park information); (906) 337-3168 (park office—for detailed operational questions)
http://www.nps.gov/kewe/

This large, rambling park is dedicated to the early days of mining on the Keweenaw Peninsula. The park includes several loosely connected sites, among the most interesting of which is the Quincy Mine Hoist and Underground Mine, where visitors can learn the story of the Quincy Mining Company and see the largest steam hoist in the world. Underground tours give a firsthand view of the copper mines, including the equipment and its use. Another site is the Hanka Homestead, an early Finnish immigrant farm, which remains much as it did at the turn of the 20th century. Many Finnish immigrants to the Keweenaw worked in the mines until they could afford to buy or homestead a small, self-sufficient farm. The Hanka Homestead preserves just such a small farm, featuring hewn log buildings in a pristine cultural landscape.

Southwestern States

Acoma Pueblo Sky City
Acoma Tourist Center
P.O. Box 309
Acoma, NM 87034
(800) 747-0181; (505) 470-4967 or 4966

Established ca. 1300 and located 12 miles east of Grants off Interstate 40, Acoma is one of the oldest continuously occupied settlements in the United States. This pueblo city sits fortresslike atop a high mesa. The residents of Acoma Pueblo have considerable interaction with neighboring non-Indians, yet maintain their identity as a separate community with distinctive cultural systems. Acoma is now home to about 570 residents. It was proclaimed a National Historic Landmark on October 9, 1960.

Western States

Petaluma Adobe State Historic Park
Mailing Address:
Silverado District Headquarters
20 East Spain St.
Sonoma, CA 95476
(707) 938-1519 or 762-4871
Follow State markers off Highway 101 and 116 east at Adobe and Casa Grande Roads

Once the largest and richest privately owned Mexican estate north of San Francisco Bay, Rancho Petaluma was built by General Mariano Guadalupe Vallejo during the rancho era, 1834–44. Visitors can see authentic hand tools, authentic furnishings, interpretive displays, and domestic animals that make it possible to visualize many aspects of life on Vallejo's sprawling rancho. Vallejo spent only some of his time at Petaluma Adobe, however, and to get the full picture, visitors should also stop at nearby Sonoma State Historic Park.

Sonoma State Historic Park

Silverado District Headquarters
20 East Spain Street
Sonoma, CA 95476
(707) 938-1519

Sonoma State Historic Park consists of several restored buildings that date back to the earliest days of the Mexican era and the beginnings of California's incorporation into the United States. Around the town's central plaza, visitors can visit historic structures that include the Mission San Francisco Solano de Sonoma, a site selected and consecrated by Father José Altimira on July 4, 1823; the Blue Wing Inn, a gambling room and saloon of the gold rush era; and the Sonoma Barracks, a two-story, wide-balconied, adobe barracks built to house Mexican army troops under the command of General Vallejo, who moved his troops from San Francisco to Sonoma in 1834. From then until 1846, Sonoma was the headquarters of the commandant of the Frontera del Norte—the Mexican provincial frontier of the north.

Other structures include the Toscano Hotel, probably constructed during the 1850s, and La Casa Grande, General Vallejo's first home. La Casa Grande, one of the most imposing and well-furnished private residences in California, stood in the middle of the block with its wide second-story balcony overlooking the plaza. La Casa Grande soon became the center of social and diplomatic life north of San Francisco Bay. It was in La Casa Grande on the morning of June 14, 1846, that the general, his brother Salvador, and his brother-in-law Jacob Leese were confronted by leaders of the insurgent Bear Flag Party—following several hours of negotiations, the three men were taken prisoner and sent to Sutter's Fort for detention. Their captors then declared the end of Mexican rule in California.

MORE READING SOURCES

I n addition to the suggested readings at the end of each chapter of this book, the following list provides additional suggestions for exploring further.

Anderson, Joan. *Pioneer Children of Appalachia*. Photographs by George Ancona. New York: Clarion Books, 1986.

Athearn, Robert. *In Search of Canaan: Black Migration to Kansas, 1879–80*. Lawrence: University Press of Kansas, 1978.

"Deerfield Issue," *Cobblestone Magazine*. (September 1995).

Demos, John. *The Unredeemed Captive: A Family Story from Early America*. New York: Knopf, 1994.

Dolan, Sean. *James Beckwourth, Frontiersman*. New York: Chelsea House, 1992.

Editors of *Sunset*. *The California Missions: A Pictorial History*. Menlo Park, Calif.: Lane Publishing, 1979.

Editors of Time-Life Books. *The Frontiersmen*. With text by Paul O'Neil. Alexandria, Va.: Time-Life Books, 1977.

Fox, Mary Virginia. *The Story of Women Who Shaped the West*. Chicago: Childrens Press, 1991.

Fulton, Arabella. *A Pioneer Woman's Memoir: Based on the Journal of Arabella Clemens Fulton*. Edited by Judith E. Greenberg and Helen Carey McKeever. New York: Franklin Watts, 1995.

Gillenkirk, Jeff, and James Motlow. *Bitter Melon: Inside America's Last Rural Chinese Town*. Berkeley: Heyday Books, 1993.

Lawlor, Laurie. *Daniel Boone*. Illustrated by Bert Dodson. Niles, Ill.: A. Whitman, 1989.

Lyngheim, Linda. *Father Junipero Serra: The Traveling Missionary*. Van Nuys, Calif.: Langtry Publications, 1986.

———. *The Indians and the California Missions*. Illustrated by Phyllis Garber. Van Nuys, Calif.: Langtry Publications, 1984.

Melvoin, Richard I. *New England Outpost: War and Society in Colonial Deerfield*. New York: Norton, 1989.

Miller, Brandon Marie. *Buffalo Gals: Women of the Old West*. Minneapolis: Lerner Publications, 1995.

Miller, Luree, and Scott Miller. *Alaska: Pioneer Stories of a Twentieth-Century Frontier*. New York: Cobblehill Books, 1991.

Nobles, Gregory H. *American Frontiers: Cultural Encounters and Continental Conquest*. First Hill & Wang edition. New York: Hill & Wang, 1997.

Notson, Adelia White, and Robert Carver Notson, editors. *Stepping Stones: The Pilgrim's Own Story*. Portland, Oreg.: Binford & Mort Publishing, 1987.

Painter, Nell. *Exodusters: Black Migration to Kansas after Reconstruction*. Lawrence: University Press of Kansas, 1986.

INDEX

Boldface page references indicate main headings. *Italic* page references indicate illustrations. The letter *m* following a page reference indicates a map or diagram.

Illinois xiv
Independence, Missouri 89, 110
Indian Wars
    ended at Fort Bowie 98
    Santa Fe Trail 89, 92, 93–94
    Seminole 21
intermarriage 79
International Falls, Minnesota 58
irrigation 45–46

J

Jamestown colony xiv, 16
Jefferds Tavern 125
Jefferson, Thomas 62, 63–66
Jefferson National Expansion Memorial 71
Jenkins Hill (Lookout Hill) 90
Jenner, California 74–84
John Hancock Warehouse 125
Johnson, Nels 113, 119
Johnson Pioneer Cabin Site 119
Jorgensen, Jorgen 119
Junction, Utah 114
Juno (ship) 77

K

Kansas 87–98
Kashaya Pomo Indians 75, 79
Keweenaw National Historical Park **130**
Kiksadi Fort 85
kiva 1, 3, *4*, 6–9
Kodiak Island 76, 79
Kuskov, Ivan 77–79
Kuskov House 81

L

La Casa Grande (Vallejo's house) 132
Lachine Rapids 57
La Habaña, Cuba 20, 21
La Junta, Colorado 89
Lake Superior 50, 52, 59–60
land bridge, Siberia to Alaska xiii
Larned, Benjamin F. 90
Larned, Kansas 87–98
Leese, Jacob 132
Le Moyne, Pierre, Sieur d'Iberville 30
Lewis, Meriwether xiv–xv, 62, 63, 65, 66–67,
    68. *See also* Lewis and Clark expedition
Lewis and Clark expedition xiv–xv, 61–73

background 64–66
daily life 66, 67, 68
map 63
salt-making activities 61, 69–70
scientific findings 70
trail retracing 71–72
Lewis and Clark National Historic Trail **71–72**
Lewis and Clark River 67
Lewis and Clark Trail Heritage Foundation 72
lighthouses
    Apostle Island National Lakeshore,
        Wisconsin 59, 60
    Pemaquid Point, Maine 36
Little Sand Bay 59, 60
Little Women (film) 123
Lolo Pass 71
Lookout Hill (Jenkins Hill) 90
"Lost colony" (Roanoke Island) xiv, 16, 22,
    128
Lost Colony, The (outdoor drama) 128
Louisiana xiv, 64
Louisiana Purchase (1803) xiv–xv, 62, 63–65

M

Mackenzie, Alexander 51
Maine
    Old York Historic District 124–25
    Pemaquid settlement xiv, 25–36
Maine Bureau of Parks and Recreation 34
Mangas Coloradas 98
Manteo, North Carolina 128
Margil de Jesús, Fray Antonio 40
marine hunting 79–80
Marshall, James 111
Marshall Gold Discovery State Historic Park
    111
masonry 5, 6
Massachusetts 123, 124
Massachusetts Bay Colony 27, 28, 29, 30
Matanzas River 15, 24
Menéndez de Avilés, Pedro 15, 16, 22
Merin Smith Shed and Blacksmith Shop 119
Mesa Verde Anasazi culture 1, 3
Mesa Verde National Park **12**
Mexican rancho era (California) 131, 132
Mexican War (1846–48) 89
Mey, Cornelius Jacobsen 125
Michigan 60, 130
Micmac Indians 27
military posts. *See* forts